RUSSIAN SCIENCE FICTION FILMS (FILM GUIDE)

Books LLC®, Reference Series, Memphis, USA, 2011. www.booksllc.net. Copyright: http://creativecommons.org/licenses/by-sa/3.0/deed.en

Table of Contents

Russian science fiction films
Alice's Birthday 1
First on the Moon 2
Paragraph 78 3
Star Wars: Storm in the Glass 3
The Inhabited Island 5

Soviet science fiction films
Aelita 7
Aerograd 7
Amphibian Man (film) 7
Battle Beyond the Sun 8
Contact (animated short film) 8

Dead Man's Letters 8
Failure of Engineer Garin 9
Guest from the Future 9
Heart of a Dog (film) 11
Ivan Vasilievich: Back to the Future. 12
Kin-dza-dza! 13
Kosmicheskiy reys 15
Moscow-Cassiopeia 16
Mysterious Island (1941 film) 16
New Adventures of a Yankee in King Arthur's Court 17
Per Aspera Ad Astra (film) 17
Polygon (film) 18

Solaris (1968 film) 18
Solaris (1972 film) 18
Stalker (film) 22
Teens in the Universe 27
Test pilota Pirxa 27
The Adventures of the Elektronic 28
The Andromeda Nebula 29
The Hyperboloid of Engineer Garin (film) 29
The Mystery of the Third Planet 29
The Sannikov Land (film) 30
The Witches Cave 30

Introduction

Purchase of this book entitles you to a free trial membership in the publisher's book club at www.booksllc.net. (Time limited offer.) Simply enter the barcode number from the back cover onto the membership form. The book club entitles you to select from hundreds of thousands of books at no additional charge. You can also download a digital copy of this and related books to read on the go. Simply enter the title or subject onto the search form to find them.

Each chapter in this book ends with a URL to a hyperlinked online version. Type the URL exactly as it appears. If you change the URL's capitalization it won't work. Use the online version to access related pages, websites, footnotes, tables, color photos, updates. Click the version history tab to see the chapter's contributors. Click the edit link to suggest changes.

A large and diverse editor base collaboratively wrote the book, not a single author. After a long process of discussion and debate, the chapters gradually took on a neutral point of view reached through consensus. Additional editors expanded and contributed to chapters striving to achieve balance and comprehensive coverage. This reduced the regional or cultural bias found in many other books and provided access and breadth on subject matter otherwise little documented.

Alice's Birthday

Alice's Birthday (Russian: День рождения Али́сы, translit. Den' rozhdeniya Alisy), is a 2009 Russian animated feature film directed by Sergey Seryogin and produced by Master-film studio. The animated film is based on a story by Kir Bulychyov about Alisa (Alice) Seleznyova, a young girl living in the second half of the 21st century. It is the third animation to be based on one of the Alice stories, with the first having been *The Mystery of the Third Planet* (1981).

Roughly one third of the film's 60 million ruble budget was provided by the Russian government.

The film premiered in Star City, Russia on February 12, 2009. It was widely released in Russia on February 19 with 250 film prints.

Some of the scenes were done using Flash animation. The part of Gromozeka was played by Aleksey Kolgan, who is also the Russian voice of Shrek.. Natalya Guseva, who played "Alice" in a famous earlier live-action series, has a minor role as the spaceship captain.

Script Editor - Natalya Abramova.
Art Director - Sergey Gavrilov.

Background

The story "Alice's Birthday" was written by Kir Bulychev in 1971, and published in 1974 in the book *Girl from Earth* (Russian: Девочка с Земли).

Cast

- Yasya Nikolayeva as Alice
- Yevgeniy Stychkin as Professor R-r-

- r
- Aleksey Kolgan as Gromozeka
- Roman Staburov as Doctor/Stepan
- Svetlana Svetikova as singer
- Natalya Guseva as Spaceship captain
- Mark Chernavin as Bolo
- Nikolai Lazarev as Professor Seleznyov

Source (edited): "http://en.wikipedia.org/wiki/Alice%27s_Birthday"

First on the Moon

For the science fiction novel by Hugh Walters, see First on the Moon (book)
First on the Moon (Russian: Первые на Луне, *Pervye na Lune*) is a 2005 Russian mockumentary about a 1930s Soviet landing on the Moon. The film, which went on to win many awards, was the debut of the director Aleksey Fedorchenko.

The film is not related to the actual Soviet Moonshot program.

Plot

A group of journalists are investigating a highly secret document when they uncover a sensational story: that even before the Second World War, in 1938, the first rocket was made in the USSR and Soviet scientists were planning to send an orbiter to the moon and back. The evidence is convincing; it is clear that in this case, Soviet cosmonauts were first.

The film's story stretches across a broad swath of time (from the Middle Ages to the modern day) and geography (Russia, Ukraine, Malaysia, Polynesia, Chile).

The movie follows the selection and training of a small group of cosmonauts. The cosmonaut who shines above the others (similar to the clear front-runners in the early historical Soviet space program) is Captain Ivan Sergeyevich Kharlamov (spelled Harlamov in the subtitles). He is helped into a space suit and loaded into the capsule, and the rocket lifts off for the Moon—but contact with it is soon lost.

Most of the remainder of the film seems to follow the search for information about what happened next, as the 1930s space program appears to have dissolved immediately after, but with no reason given (but presumably as a part of Stalin's purges). It is implied that Kharlamov returned to Earth, but with no fanfare and apparently no assistance from the space program. A number of men are shown as suspected of being Kharlamov—the NKVD seems to be conducting a criminal investigation of the program and it is implied that those involved, including Kharlamov himself, are in hiding.

It is implied that the capsule returned to Earth and landed in Chile, and that Kharlamov journeyed to the Soviet Far East by way of Polynesia and China, yet feared capture on his return. His wife (widow?) seems to have covered for him when interrogated as to his whereabouts. The narrator never ties the story together coherently, however; the interviews and footage are shown without supporting commentary, in a (non)narration style reminiscent of an actual documentary of the Soviet lunar program, *The Red Stuff*.

The very end of the movie shows the only footage of the mission itself after launch, a film which was found at the Chilean landing site and is currently in the possession of "the Natural museum in the town of Antafagasta". First there is a brief clip showing Kharlamov piloting the vehicle, presumably on final approach to the Moon (a still from which is featured on the movie's cover). Following that is an equally brief panorama of a lunar landscape with the capsule or lander (it's unclear whether this was a direct ascent Moon landing) resting on the surface, apparently taken by Kharlamov during lunar EVA. Then there is a short clip of the other cosmonauts walking through a hangar with the 1930s space program director, and the credits roll.

Filming

The cosmonaut space training was filmed in Chelyabinsk, at the Institute of Aviation, where there exists equipment from Star City which even Gagarin used for training. The actors worked without stunt doubles; they were really spinning in the centrifuge, despite the fact that this training is difficult even for professionals.

Reaction

When elements of the plot started leaking out, a number of Russian newspapers treated it as a documentary about a real 1938 event, referring to it as the Santiago Meteorite (метеорит "Сантьяго"). In reality, the film is a falsification from beginning to end. To quote the director: "Some type of new genre. It was very difficult to decide on a name. So far, for me this is either historical drama or documentary fantasy." He also said: "Our film is about how the Soviet state machinery manufactured major products - the best people. Fine, strong and clever heroes, then rendered [them] unnecessary to the native land – some have been destroyed, others lost in obscurity, yet others still broken by fear."

Technical details

- Black and White and Color, 75 minutes
- Director: Aleksey Fedorchenko
- Screenplay: Aleksandr Gonorovskiy and Ramil Yamaleyev
- Cinematography: Anatoliy Lesnikov
- Set Designs: Nikolay Pavlov
- Cast: Boris Vlasov, Aleksey Slavnin, Andrey Osipov, Anatoliy Otradnov, Viktoriya Ilinskaya.
- Producers: Dmitriy Vorobyov and Aleksey Fedorchenko
- Production: Sverdlovsk Film Studio and Film Company Strana

In numbers

- Work on the film took three years
- The budget was $1 million
- The rocket built for the film was 80 meters long
- 1000 people took part in the film

Awards

- 2005—Cottbus Film Festival of Young East European Cinema: First Work Award of the Student Jury and Special Prize
- 2005—Flanders International Film Festival: Grand Prix
- 2005—Venice Film Festival: Venice Horizons Documentary Award
- 2005—Warsaw International Film Festival: Special Mention
- 2005—Zagreb Film Festival: "Golden Pram" award
- 2005— "The best debut" prize, Kinotaur festival, Sochi, Russia
- 2006—Eurocon: Best performance

Source (edited): "http://en.wikipedia.org/wiki/First_on_the_Moon"

Paragraph 78

Paragraph 78 (screen name - *§ 78*) is a Russian film by Mikhail Khleborodov released in 2007. Film was split into two parts **Paragraph 78, Punkt 1** released February 22, 2007 and **Paragraph 78, Punkt 2** released March 29, 2007.

The screenplay was based on a 1995 story by Ivan Ohlobystin.

Andrey Lazarchuk, Russian writer of the modern turborealism literature style, wrote a novel based on this film (February 2007).

Plot

Future: soft drugs are legalized, countries such as the Asian Union and the Latin States of America appeared. An assault group under the command of Gudvin (Gosha Kutsenko) breaks apart because of his conflict with Skif (Vladimir Vdovichenkov).

Five years later Lisa (Anastasiya Slanevskaya) left Skif and is married to Gudvin. Russia, the Asian Union and the Latin States watch closely after each other's WMD production cessation.

A state of emergency declared at one of the secret and per international treaty prohibited laboratories of the Russian Ministry of Defense on an island in the Arctic Ocean causes an emergency beacon to start to operate. Now the other countries can possibly locate this base. To prevent this from happening Gudvin assembles his former group. By that time Spam (Anatoli Belyj) is jailed, Luba (Stanislav Duzhnikov) works in that same prison as a warden, Festival (Grigori Siyatvinda) is engaged in commerce of banned drugs (lysergic acid), Pai (Azis Beyshinaliev) works in a casino, Skif ruins himself with drink.

Together they depart to that island to penetrate the base and stop the emergency beacon.

Cast

- Gosha Kutsenko as Gudvin
- Vladimir Vdovichenkov as Skif
- Grigori Siyatvinda as Festival
- Anastasiya Slanevskaya as Lisa
- Stanislav Duzhnikov as Luba
- Azis Beyshinaliev as Pai
- Anatoli Belyj as Spam
- Yusup Bakshiyev as Doktor
- Mikhail Yefremov as Prison commander
- The film was heavily criticised for strong resemblance to a number of films, including *Resident Evil*, *Doom*, *Phantom Force*, *Dragon Fighter*, and *Aliens*.
- The film was heavily packed by product placement as the recent Russian films *Night Watch* and *Day Watch*. This includes Russian Channel One, *Fan* chips, Men's Health magazine, Pikador ketchup, Mail.ru service, *Radio Maximum*, *Golden barrel* beer, *Grand Prix* vodka, Wrigley's Spearmint, Qtek S110, Creative player, Panasonic notebook, etc.
- Some critics noted the biggest "trickery" of the audience in the history of Russian film industry because the film was broken up in two parts at a cliffhanger.

Source (edited): "http://en.wikipedia.org/wiki/Paragraph_78"

Star Wars: Storm in the Glass

Star Wars: Storm in the Glass (Russian: Звёздные войны: Буря в стакане, refers to operation of Persian Gulf War "Desert Storm"), sometimes translated as *Star Wars: Tempest in a Teapot*, is a humorous 2004 English-to-Russian movie spoof of the 1999 science fantasy film *Star Wars Episode I: The Phantom Menace* by popular Russian movie translator Dmitry "Goblin" Puchkov. In dubbing the film into Russian, Puchkov altered the plotline, character names, music, and certain visual effects to provide a different (and funny) experience to Russian-speaking audiences.

Synopsis

The operational conditions on the boundless open spaces of the Far-Northern Galaxy have rapidly become complicated. On secret planets, persons of unknown nationality (a reference to many Georgian-Armenian and Moldovan illegal immigrants in Russia) have set up manufacture of illegal alcohol on a galactic scale and are preparing an act of aggression against the peaceful planet Marabu.

To carry out a series of covert search missions the command sends two jedi - experienced workers of the Special Hare Krishna sect. As their first step in solving the problem, the jedi land on a space-station of the alcohol pirates to investigate, but they are ambushed and forced to battle their way out through various silly robots and kolobkis (Kolobok is a fictional Russian children's story character).By the time the heroes escape from the space-station and reach the capital with the help of a local Chukchi rapper, the angry bourgeois occupy the peaceful planet.

The jedi rescue the queen Zadolbala and escape on a stolen pepelats (an homage to a Russian film *Kin-dza-dza!*). During their escape, the spacecraft is damaged and heroically fixed in-flight by Vedroid ("Bucket Droid") model E2-E4 (), and are forced to make a landing on the planet Babooine (which carries many references to Iraq and the Second Gulf War). While visiting the store of a local Jewish Mossad trader, the jedi and the rapper meet a local boy, Anykey Skovorodker ("Skillet man") whose father was also rumored to be a jedi. To aid his father's coworkers, Anykey takes part in the Crazy Taxi Races , (a reference to a driving manner of many Russian share taxi drivers), during which he is nearly beaten by Grytsko Schumacher. On Babooin, the jedi also fight Javded (a strange man with red skin and small horns, who attacked the jedi after not being satisfied by them not wearing any hats.

After failing to sway the politicians of the galactic Duma (Russian Senate), the queen of Marabu develops a plan for operation "Storm in a Glass" (a play on "Operation Storm in the Desert"; also the Russian idiomatic equivalent to "Tempest in a Teapot"). Two divisions of underwater deer-herders, hidden in a fighter Anykey - everything sets up against the provisional government of bourgeois and their army of electronic dummies. During one of the fights, the jedi once again meet with the "red unmannered man" who attacks them once again (supposedly) for not wearing any hats. He is behalved and his lower half of the body (lower abdomen and legs) are identified, while it is a mystery to whom the other half belongs. Only in the "God's Spark" version of the film does it become clear who is Anykey's real father - it is Pogon, who admits to have "known" (commonly understood as "have/d sex with") Anykey's mother, and later openly explains that Anykey is his only son.

- **Pogon** (Russian for "rank insignia") - one of two jedi sent to Marabu. Original: Qui-Gon Jinn
- **Pavian iz Nairobi** (Russian for "baboon from Nairobi") - padavan-jedi sent to Marabu. Original: Obi-Wan Kenobi
- **Djaga-Djaga Bzdinks** (refers to the chorus of Katya Lel's top chart song *Moy Marmeladny*) - Chukchi rapper exiled from the underwater sovkhoz, whose other inhabitants can't stand hip-hop. Likes to call himself "Wise Scarecrow". Original: Jar-Jar Binks
- **"Slimy Swamp Toad"** (nicknamed so by surface-dwellers) - chairman of the "Underwater Deer" sovkhoz, likes scuba diving and hates hip-hop. Original: Boss Nass
- **Queen Zadolbala** (Russian slang meaning "sick of [her]") - rightful ruler of planet Marabu. Rumored to be a blow-up doll. Original: Handmaiden Sabé
- **Maid Padla** (Russian slang meaning "bastard") - servant girl of Queen Zadolbala, a former Playboy playmate. Original: Padmé Amidala
- **Poruchik Rzhevsky** (subject of many Russian jokes) - head of the queen's guard. Original: Captain Panaka
- **E2-E4** (common opening move in chess) - repair bucketdroid (AKA bucket with eyes), good at fixing oil leaks. Original: R2-D2
- **Robot Chatterbird** (refers to the talking bird in *The Mystery of the Third Planet*) - robot specializes in poor film translations, capable of understanding E2-E4. His voice is a gag on Leonid Volodarskiy Original: C-3PO
- **Anykey Skovorodker** (first name refers to "press any key..."; last name comes from "skovorodka" - Russian for "frying pan") - young boy, works in a mechanical shop. His father is rumored to be a jedi. Original: Anakin Skywalker
- **Boris Abramovich** (refers to Boris Abramovich Berezovsky, a Russian billionaire) - Jewish trader of mechanical parts, Anykey's boss; has connections to the Mossad. Original: Watto
- **Valeria Ilyinichna Novodvorskaya** (obese Russian famous democrate female politician, anti-communist, call herself a liberal, has pro-Western views) - pro-democratic political activist invited to start off the Crazy Taxi Races. Original: Jabba the Hutt
- **Grytsko Schumacher** ("Grytsko" is a common Ukrainian name; Michael Schumacher was a famous Formula One racer) - cheating racer at the Crazy Taxi Races, likes eating uncooked chicken. Original: Sebulba
- **Darth bin Laden** (refers to Osama bin Laden) - shadowy figure behind the illegal alcohol manufacture and invasion of Marabu. Original: Darth Sidious
- **Javdeth** (refers to never appeared character of the extremely popular soviet movie *White Sun of the Desert* - a coward and the mortal enemy of Sayid) - loyal follower of Darth bin Laden, experienced swordfighter. Hates women after his ex-wife cheated on him (reference to his horns). Original: Darth Maul
- **Boris Nikolayevich** (refers to Boris Nikolayevich Yeltsin - former president of Russia) - speaker of the Galactic Duma, impeached for heavy drinking at Queen Zadolbala's request. Original: Finis Valorum
- **Cheburan Vissarionovich** (refers to Cheburashka - a popular Russian fairy tale creature; could also refer to the "Buran" spacecraft; the second name is a reference to Joseph Stalin) - old miser in charge of the Krishna operative school. Original: Yoda

Planets

- **Marabu** (reference to the Marabou Stork) - planet in the Far-Northern Galaxy, contains a city populated by surface-dwellers and an underwater sovkhoz populated by the Chukchi people. Original: Naboo
- **Planet of the State Duma** - capital planet of the Republic, featuring the planet-wide city of **Washingtonsk**. Features flying trains, the waving Statue of Liberty, and an eye-like projector on top of the Jedi tower. Original: Coruscant
- **Babooine** - desert world populated by slave-traders, maniacs, prostitutes, Mujahideen of Ahmad Shah Massoud, and other fine citizens of

the galaxy. Occasional American helicopters can be seen blowing up cattle for no apparent reason. Original: Tatooine
- **Baghdad** - Anykey's hometown on Babooine. The town center features a large portrait of Saddam Hussein. Place of the planet-famous Crazy Taxi Races. Original: Mos Espa
- **Mars** - an arid world populated by American robots.

Other replacements
- **The Crimson Jihad** (from the film *True Lies*) is the organization sponsoring the invasion. Their signature music is the *Prince of Persia: The Sands of Time* soundtrack ("Prelude Fight") overlaid with a Muezzin call. Original: The Trade Federation
- The Jihad is controlled by the Rubber Faces (refers to the "man in a rubber suit" concept of earlier sci-fi films). Original: Neimoidians

Trivia
- This is the first Goblin's humorous translation that contains added/modified graphics. The most common addition is a bottle of vodka on almost every table. Also, Neo can be seen flying by during the Crazy Taxi Races.
- The translation makes numerous references to the Russian science-fiction film *Kin-dza-dza!*
- The parade scene at the end features a Yoda-like George W. Bush standing near Yoda. Goblin himself can be seen standing behind Mace Windu in the same scene.

Source (edited): "http://en.wikipedia.org/wiki/Star_Wars:_Storm_in_the_Glass"

The Inhabited Island

The Inhabited Island (Russian: Обитаемый остров) is a 2008-2009 science fiction film directed by Fyodor Bondarchuk based on a 1971 novel by Arkady and Boris Strugatsky of the same Russian name, published in English as *Prisoners of Power*. Due to the length of the filmed material, the film is being released in two installments. The first movie was released in Russia on December 18, 2008 and the conclusion released on April 23, 2009.

Plot summary

Part I

In the year 2157, the main character, Maxim Kammerer (Stepanov), is a space pilot of the *Free Search Group*. His spaceship is damaged and he crash lands on an unknown planet. The ship is destroyed just after Maxim crawls out of it. Maxim is discovered and arrested by Zef (Garmash), a native of the planet. Guy Gaal (Fyodorov), a Corporal of the Guards, is appointed to escort him to the military camp.

As they are making their way to the capital by rail, their military convoy is attacked by so-called "degenerates". The degenerates destroy a nearby tower, which is said to be part of a ballistic missile defense. Maxim demonstrates great physical prowess during the attack and saves Guy from imminent death. Maxim learns that the name of the planet is Saraksh, and the country where he landed is governed by a militaristic dictatorship of the *Unknown Fathers*.

Maxim is in the process of being escorted to Strannik (Wanderer in Russian), a powerful figure in the government; but one of Strannik's men, Fank, suffers from a surge of epilepsy, Maxim is able to escape. He encounters Rada Gaal (Snigir), a sister of Guy, and falls in love with her. Maxim stays in the city with Guy and Rada and gets conscripted into the Guards. He learns about the ongoing war and tries to determine who exactly the enemy is and what they are fighting for. After Maxim refuses to execute a group of captured degenerates, he is shot by his superior and left to die.

Nevertheless, Maxim recovers and joins a group of degenerate fighters. During his time with the degenerates, Maxim learns the true nature of the towers erected across the country. Contrary to the state propaganda, the towers actually function as mind control devices, sending a special kind of radiation that ensures the citizens' loyalty to the state. Two times a day, the majority of the country's population experiences a patriotic frenzy but the remainder suffers from intense pain and convulsions. It seems like the degenerates, as well as the Unknown Fathers, are the minority which do not submit to the towers' radiation, though they suffer from excruciating pain at the time of radiation spikes.

The degenerates do not actually seek to dismantle the system of towers, but plan to overthrow the Unknown Fathers and use the mind control system for their own designs. Both the degenerates and the Fathers seek to recruit Maxim, since he is immune both to mind control and pain, but he decides that neither the degenerates nor the Fathers deserve his allegiance.

After fighting alongside the degenerates in the attack on a tower, Maxim is again captured by the military and sentenced to a prison labor camp tasked with cleaning minefields. When on mission, Maxim and two other prisoners, Zef and Veper, find an abandoned power transmission station in the woods. While exploring the underground floor, they encounter the golovans, a race of seemingly wild dog-like creatures who attack the prisoners. Maxim speculates that they may be sentient and highly intelligent.

As they exit the station, Maxim manages to capture a mechanized tank which attacked the prisoners in the woods. He drives the tank to the border where he again encounters Guy who is serving at a border post. Maxim takes Guy with him and heads south to the neighbouring nations.

Part II

The second part is named *Skhvatka*

(*Skirmish*); it starts with a brief description of the first part plot.

Maxim tries to reveal the true purpose of the towers to Guy, who does not believe at first but is convinced when his enthusiasm fades considerably as they get farther from the coverage area of the towers.

They arrive in the once-prosperous part of the empire, now turned a God-forsaken desert in an aftermath of an atomic war. They meet the mutant people who are suffering from the effects of radiation poisoning and are pursued by both the border guards and the barbarians from the south. Maxim tries to convince mutants to start a rebellion or join the barbarians to fight with the so-called *Fatherland*, but they are too weak both physically and morally.

They advise him to ask help from *The Wizard*, a mutant kid with paranormal abilities. Maxim laments if it is at all possible to overtake the regime of the Fathers, but finally decides to join the Islands Empire to fight the Unknown Fathers. A leader of the mutants, who is a former Colonel of the medical service, convinces Maxim that a desert passage would be too dangerous and presents him with a flying bomber-airship that survived the war.

As Guy and Maxim fly the airship, Guy falls victim to the tower radiation that reaches them and shows his fanatical allegiance, this time to Maxim personally. Maxim collides the airship into the Tower and destroys it, but the airship is shot down by automatic anti-aircraft guns.

After crash-landing in the sea, Maxim and Guy successfully reach ground and find an abandoned Imperial White Submarine. They find evidence of mass killings in the Islands Empire and it is now crystal clear that joining the Islands Empire is impossible.

Meanwhile, the State Prosecutor makes plans to find Maxim and use his outstanding abilities for his profit. He talks with Rada but after she declines his request to cooperate, puts her in jail. Strannik helps Rada escape the Prosecutor since he also wants to find Maxim.

Maxim learns that the Fatherland declared war on Khonti, former part of the united Empire, and he and Guy surrender to a land patrol. They and most of the male prisoners are sent to the front, including his friends Zef and Veper. During the battle Guy perishes. Fank finds Maxim and convinces him to join Strannik's quarters.

Fatherland is quickly defeated, and the State Prosecutor, who was an active supporter of the war, realizes that the Unknown Fathers will assassinate him for this failure. He contacts Maxim and reveals the location of the Tower Control Center, wanting him to destroy it. Maxim concurs with his reasoning and destroys the Center with the help of Resistance leaders Zef and Veper, then saves Rada from Strannik.

Strannik realizes what has happened but only when it is too late. He chases Maxim and during their final confrontation it is revealed that Strannik's real name is Rudolf Sikorski and he is from Earth as well. Sikorski works in the Galactic Security Bureau and he was the President of Earth for some time. Sikorski blames Maxim with spoiling a thoroughly prepared plan to save this planet. He reminds Maxim about movable radiators which are functionally equivalent to the Towers, the imminent starvation, the raising inflation, the need for economic recovery and for decontamination of radioactive lands.

Strannik also reveals that the Islands Empire plans an invasion to the Fatherland, which would be very hard to counteract without the so-called *black radiation* of the Towers, which causes depression. He suggests Maxim to return home to Earth.

Maxim responds that this planet is his home and his primary objective is to not allow anybody to rebuild the *zombie towers*, but he is ready to cooperate with Sikorski on other matters. Sikorski agrees to this, and Maxim stays on the planet with Rada.

Cast

- Vasiliy Stepanov as *Maxim Kammerer* (voiced by Maksim Matveev)
- Yuliya Snigir as *Rada Gaal*
- Pyotr Fyodorov as *Guy Gaal*
- Aleksei Serebryakov as *Strider*
- Fyodor Bondarchuk as *State Prosecutor* aka *Smart*
- Sergey Garmash as *Zef*
- Gosha Kutsenko as *Veper*
- Andrei Merzlikin as *Fank*
- Mikhail Yevlanov as *Rittmeister Chachu*
- Anna Mikhalkova as *Ordi Tader*
- Sergei Barkovsky as *Nolle Renadu*
- Aleksey Gorbunov as *Shurin*
- Maksim Sukhanov as *Dad*
- Yuriy Tsurilo as the *General*
- Aleksandr Feklistov as *Dever*
- Kirill Pirogov as *Svyokor*
- Yevgeni Sidikhin as *Teste*
- Sergei Mazayev as *Voldyr*
- Leonid Gromov as *Gramenau*
- Vasili Savinov as *Lesnik*
- Vyacheslav Razbegayev as *Krysolov*
- Dimash Akhimov as *Behemoth*
- Ignat Akrachkov as *Prosecutor's referent*

Production

The film is a production of Art Pictures Studio, Non-Stop Productions and Russian STS Channel, with special effects by EyeScream Studio, Main Road Post and Quantum Creation FX.

The production was filmed in Crimea, Ukraine, with photography lasting for 10 months (February 14 - December 7, 2007). The film had a total budget of about $36.6 million, including $10 million for the film's promotion and $1 million of state donations.It the biggest budget Russian film ever made in the Russian Federation weighing in at $36.6 million and beating fellow Russian Blockbuster The Admiral which weighed in at $20 million.

Reception

The Inhabited Island was met with mixed reviews. Most praised the film for being surprisingly faithful to the novel. Some praised the film's visual effects, while others criticized the work of director and editor. Mir Fantastiki review called the film a "chaotic mash of visual, dramatical and musical components, each of which separately has quite high quality". "The movie scatters into a mosaic of spectacular images, that don't comprise the consistent image of the world", agrees Total DVD

Film was a relative commercial failure. Despite grossing around $30 mln from two parts summarily and ranking among the top-grossing films of Russia's modern cinema, it didn't repay its budget of $36 mln. The movie was released on DVD very shortly after it exited theatres, in the hope of covering the debt.

Boris Strugatsky, the only living of the book's co-authors, said the film is a "directors' success", noting its faithfulness to the novel. He praised the work of Serebryakov (Strannik), Bondarchuk (Umnik) and Garmash (Zef), but expressed disappointment over the work of Kutsenko (Vepr'), Mikhalkova (Ordi Tader) and Merzlikin (Funk). He noted Stepanov as one of the biggest success of the film, saying that "Maxim Kammerer is exactly as we imagined him".
Source (edited): "http://en.wikipedia.org/wiki/The_Inhabited_Island"

Aelita

Aelita (Russian: Аэлита), also known as *Aelita: Queen of Mars*, is a silent film directed by Soviet filmmaker Yakov Protazanov made on Mezhrabpom-Rus film studio and released in 1924. It was based on Alexei Tolstoy's novel of the same name. Mikhail Zharov and Igor Ilyinsky were cast in leading roles.

Though the main focus of the story is the daily lives of a small group of people during the post-war Soviet Union, the enduring importance of the film comes from its early science fiction elements. It primarily tells of a young man, Los (Russian: Лось, literary Elk), traveling to Mars in a rocket ship, where he leads a popular uprising against the ruling group of Elders, with the support of Queen Aelita who has fallen in love with him after watching him through a telescope.

Influences

One of the earliest full-length films about space travel, the most notable part of the film remains its remarkable constructivist Martian sets and costumes designed by Aleksandra Ekster. Their influence can be seen in a number of later films, including the *Flash Gordon* serials and probably Fritz Lang's *Metropolis* and *Woman in the Moon*. Parts of the plot were also loosely adapted for the 1951 film *Flight to Mars*.

While very popular at first, the film later fell out of favor with the Soviet government and was thus very difficult to see until after the Cold War.
Source (edited): "http://en.wikipedia.org/wiki/Aelita"

Aerograd

Aerograd (Russian: Аэроград, also referred to as *Air City* or *Frontier*), is a 1935 Soviet film by Ukrainian director Alexander Dovzhenko, a coproduction between Mosfilm and VUFKU. It is an adventure story set in the Soviet Far East in the future.

Cast

- Stepan Shagaida as Stepan Glushak
- Sergei Stolyarov as Vladimir Slushak
- Yevgeniya Melnikova
- Stepan Shkurat as Vasili Khudiakov
- G. Tsoi as Van-Lin
- N. Tabunasov as Young Chukcha
- L. Kan as Samurai
- I. Kim
- Boris Dobronravov as Aniky Shavanov
- Yelena Maksimova
- Vladimir Uralsky

Source (edited): "http://en.wikipedia.org/wiki/Aerograd"

Amphibian Man (film)

Amphibian Man (Russian: Человек-амфибия, translit. Chelovek-amfibiya) is a 1962 Soviet science fiction romance film starring Vladimir Korenev and Directed by Vladimir Chebotaryov and Gennadi Kazansky.

It is an almost fable-like story based upon the eponymous novel by Alexander Beliaev. It focuses on a boy named *Ichtyandr* who was surgically altered to survive under the sea. Unlike traditional science fiction movies of the time the film focuses much more on the concept of love won and lost. It was given the name of *Tarzan des Mers* before the estate of Edgar Rice Burroughs took exception.

The film was the leader of Soviet distribution in 1962 (65.5 million viewers). It is little-known in the West, but has become a cult classic.

Plot

The story is set in a seaside port, largely among a community of pearl fishers. The protagonist is the son of a doctor/scientist who was sometime in the past forced to save his son's life by implanting him with gills. Thus he is able to live under water, but must keep his secret from the world. The conflict arises from his falling in love with a pearl-fisher's beautiful daughter. His secret is discovered and the girl's stern father attempts to exploit Ichtyandr for his ability. Due to being kept caged under water, he loses the ability to live in the open air, and must now permanently live in the sea. Although set free, the lovers are perma-

Battle Beyond the Sun

Battle Beyond the Sun (Russian: Небо зовет, translit. Nebo zovet, lit. ***The Sky is Calling***) is a 1959 Soviet science fiction film directed by Mikhail Karyukov and Aleksandr Kozyr. It tells of the "space race", with the USSR forced into competing with the USA to become the first nation to colonize Mars. Roger Corman acquired the film for US distribution and hired a young film-school student named Francis Ford Coppola to Americanize it. In addition to preparing a dubbing script free of anti-American propaganda and supervising the dubbing, Coppola filmed a few shots of two Martian animals fighting and cut them into the Soviet material. This Americanized version was titled **Battle Beyond the Sun** and distributed by American International Pictures in 1964.

Source (edited): "http://en.wikipedia.org/wiki/Battle_Beyond_the_Sun"

Contact (animated short film)

Contact or **Kontakt** (Russian: Контакт) is an award-winning 1978 Soviet animated short film.

Plot

A painter leaves the town and walks around countryside. While he is resting on the grass, humming the melody of "Speak Softly Love" - the Love Theme From The Godfather, a large spaceship lands near him. An alien exits the spaceship, photographs the environment and tries to contact the painter by changing his appearance to resemble nearby animals and objects and by touching him. The painter is frightened and tries to run away, but becomes tired, falls from a cliff and lies on the ground, imagining that the alien is going to lock him in a cage and torture him. The alien approaches the painter and tries to hum the same melody that the painter hummed earlier - "Speak Softly Love", but makes some mistakes. The painter understands that the alien is friendly, teaches him the correct melody, and they walk away together hand in hand.

The film has no dialogue in any language. All communication is made using music, gestures and gazes; the alien also tries to communicate by shapeshifting. Director Vladimir Tarasov explored this theme of universal communication in his other films; he considered animation "the Esperanto of all mankind".

Influence and recognition

Even though *The Godfather* films were not distributed in the Soviet Union, the theme music was familiar to Soviet people thanks to this short film.

Contact received awards at the following festivals:

- XVIII Festival of science fiction films in Trieste, 1979
- VIII Festival of short and documentary films in Lille, 1979

Source (edited): "http://en.wikipedia.org/wiki/Contact_(animated_short_film)"

Dead Man's Letters

Dead Man's Letters (Russian: Письма мёртвого человека, translit. Pisma myortvogo cheloveka), also known as ***Letters from a Dead Man***, is a 1986 Soviet science fiction film directed by Konstantin Lopushansky and produced by Lenfilm studios.

Plot

DVD cover

The plot is set in a town after a nuclear war, which was caused by a computer error and the failure of the operator to prevent the missile launch — he noticed the mistake, but choked on coffee and was not able to shout respective commands in time. The town is destroyed and polluted with radioactive elements. Police curfew is established in the immediate vicinity and only healthy people are selected for admittance to the underground bunkers. The main character, played by Rolan Bykov, is a Nobel Prize in Physics laureate, who tries to survive and helps a small group of children and adults survive by staying with them in the basement of the former museum of history. He survives by writing letters in his mind to his son Eric, though it is obvious that they will never be read. The main character is very disappointed that science has led to such a disaster. Many die from the radiation. He escapes the safe bunker, returning to the dying abandoned children, taking care of them for some time and giving them hope. Eventually he dies as well. The film ends with children wandering through the uninhabited landscape, their future undefined.
Source (edited): "http://en.wikipedia.org/wiki/Dead_Man%27s_Letters"

Failure of Engineer Garin

Failure of Engineer Garin (Russian: Крах инженера Гарина, translit. Krakh inzhenera Garina) is a 1973 Soviet television film in four parts loosely based on a novel Hyperboloid of Engineer Garin («Гиперболоид инженера Гарина») by Alexei Tolstoy. Directed by Leonid Kvinikhidze, script written by Sergei Potepalov. Produced by Lenfilm by the order of Gosteleradio of USSR. Total runtime - 247 min. Editing by Alexandra Borovskaya, cinematography by Vyacheslav Fastovich. Original music score by Vladislav Uspenskiy, conductor - Yuri Serebryakov. Sound design by Galina Gorbonosova. Stage producer - Boris Bykov.

Plot summary

A Russian engineer Petr Garin possesses a unique beam-shooting weapon that can destroy any target on practically any distance. Staging his death he emigrates from Russia as a French merchant and tries to find contacts with the head of one of the largest financial trusts in Europe, Mr. Rolling. The final goal of Garin is to rule the world...

Cast

- Oleg Borisov as *Pyotr Garin*
- Aleksandr Belyavskiy as *Vasili Shelga*
- Vasili Korzun as *Rolling*
- Nonna Terentyeva as *Zoe Montrose*
- Vladimir Tatosov as *Tyklinski*
- Mikhail Volkov as *Schefer*
- Alexander Kaidanovsky as *Dr. Wolf*
- Grigori Gaj as *Reicher*
- Anatoli Shvederskiy as *Ditz*
- Algimantas Masiulis as *Schtufen*
- Ivan Kuznetsov
- Valentin Nikulin as *Portier*
- Yefim Kopelyan as *Gaston, the 'Duck nose'*
- Vitali Yushkov as *Arnoud*
- Gediminas Karka
- Sergei Svistunov
- Vladimr Kostin as *Investigator*
- Ernst Romanov as *Khlynov*
- Gennady Saifulin as *Victor Lenoir*

Source (edited): "http://en.wikipedia.org/wiki/Failure_of_Engineer_Garin"

Guest from the Future

Guest from the Future (Russian: Гостья из будущего, *Gostya iz budushchego*) is a five-part Soviet television miniseries, made at Gorky Film Studio, first aired in 1985. It is based on the novel *One Hundred Years Ahead* (Сто лет тому вперед) by Kir Bulychev.

The series starred Natalya Guseva as Alisa Seleznyova, a girl from the future that travels to the present and Aleksei Fomkin as Kolia Gerasimov, a boy from the present who travels to the future.

The series was a great success in Soviet Union and is often reaired to this day.

Plot

Part 1

Two schoolboys, Kolya and Fima, follow a mysterious strange lady to an abandoned house. When they enter the house, they find no trace of the stranger, but in the empty basement Kolya discovers a secret door that leads to a room with a technical device in it. Curious

10 - Guest from the Future

Kolya starts pressing some buttons and activates the device that "transfers" him to another place. We learn that this place is the institute for temporal research. Employees return from time travels to different periods and deliver artifacts that are inventoried by Werther, an android who holds a secret crush on the stranger whose name is Polina. Kolya sneaks around in the corridors but is ultimately caught by Werther who starts inventorying Kolya as well, assuming that he was brought in by Polina. On this occasion Kolya learns that he has actually travelled through time into the late 21st century. Werther ponders putting Kolya in the museum but then decides to send him back in time in order to cover up what he thinks to be Polina's mistake. Kolya convinces him to let him catch some sights of the future first. On his exploration, Kolya learns about teletransportation, humanoid aliens, antigravity and space flight. He also makes contact with a grandpa Pavel, a 130-years old man who is intrigued by his 1980s school uniform.

Part 2

Having reached the space port, Kolya unsuccessfully tries to get a ticket for an interplanetary flight. However, by joining a group of pupils who escort their project satellite to the launch, he manages to enter the transit area. There he witnesses how two service workers are stunned and then impersonated by two shape-shifting aliens that have emerged from a crate. Back in the waiting hall, Kolya meets grandpa Pavel again (who turns out to be Polina's future father-in-law) and tells about what he just saw, but the old man dismisses it as child's fantasies. Grandpa Pavel introduces Kolya to Prof. Seleznyov, director of the interplanetary zoo. Kolya spots the shape-shifters again. They lure grandpa Pavel away from the group, stun and impersonate him. The fake grandpa Pavel introduces the other shape-shifter to Prof. Seleznyov as a fellow scientist. The "scientist" shows conspicuos interest in a device called "myelophone", a mind-reader. Seleznyov mentions that the device is with his daughter Alisa in the interplanetary zoo. Kolya spots and awakens the real grandpa Pavel who tells him that the aliens are space pirates and that Alisa is in danger. He asks Kolya to find Alisa. In the zoo, the pirates in new disguise steal the myelophone from Alisa who tries to read animal minds. However, with the help of a man and his talking goat, Kolya can recover the device and temporarily escapes from the pirates in an air chase. He returns to the institute. While Kolya activates the time machine, Werther sacrifices himself trying to stop the pirates. Yet they use the machine to follow Kolya into the past. Meanwhile Alisa, chasing the pirates, has reached the institute and uses the time machine as well. In the 20th century, Kolya escapes while Alisa, not accustomed to 20th-century traffic, runs into a car. Kolya and Fima discuss what to do with the myelophone. The pirates install themselves in the abandoned house and wait.

Part 3

Alisa is in hospital, recovering after the accident and faking amnesia in order to hide her origin. However, she talks about dolphin languages and exotic fruits. Her roommate Yulya thinks she just makes up those stories but likes her anyway. In the night, Kolya and Fima enter the basement of the abandoned house but the entrance to the time machine is blocked. On their way back out they barely evade the pirates. Alisa finds out that Yulya attends the same school as Kolya (whom she never saw but whose data she got from the talking goat). She confesses to Yulya that she is from the future and that Kolya has taken something from her. They are interrupted by the shape-shifters posing as the doctor and "Alisa's father". When they cannot find the myelophone, the pirates leave. At dawn the girls run away from the hospital to Yulya's place. When they meet Fima, Yulya introduces Alisa to him as a friend from far away. Alisa tells Yulya that now Kolya is in danger because he has the myelophone. Yulya has their escape covered up by her grandmother. Meanwhile the boys are turning more and more paranoid and start acting like in spy movies. Fima has correctly guessed that Alisa is the Alisa from the future. One pirate comes too late to take Alisa from the hospital but manages to retrieve Yulya's address. Yulya's grandmother arranges for Alisa to be temporarily schooled in Yulya's school in order to find the right Kolya (as there are three and Alisa does not know his family name). She also brushes off the pirate who comes to ask for the girls. The pirates decide to surveil both Yulya's place and her school.

Part 4

Alisa is admitted to school, excels in English class and also receives love letters from boys. Fima, triumphant that his predictions have come true so far, wonders whether Alisa will try to eliminate Kolya as witness if he gives her the myelophone. He explains to Kolya the danger of creating alternative timelines by using knowledge from the future. The pirates and the girls spot each other in a pedestrian precinct. A chase ensues but a neighbour with a big dog scares away the pirate. In class, the girls start interrogating the three Kolyas. The right Kolya is scared but is saved by Fima distracting the girls with a story of being in love. In a park, Kolya hides from a pirate. At home, the girls wonder why none of the Kolyas seemed to be the right one. Later the pirates observe the children during sports. Alisa exceeds in long jump, sparking interest not only in the pirates but also in a talent scout. The pirates decide to kidnap Alisa but the girls see their reflection in a shop window. They run away but are stopped by the talent scout who demands to see more of Alisa's abilities. When the girls finally arrive home, they find themselves sieged by the pirates. They disguise as an adult to leave the house on the next morning. In the park, the pirates approach one of the Kolyas but he annoys them by being overly talkative. They trick another classmate into showing them the school's back entrance. Meanwhile Kolya has picked up the myelophone from home and sneaks it in Yulya's schoolbag. A pirate enters the class disguised as teacher and calls out Alisa to check her schoolbag. When the real teacher encounters her copy, she drops unconsciuos. Kolya confesses to Alisa that he is the one who took the myelophone and runs away, distracting the pirates' attention from Alisa. After a long chase, Kolya is caught, stunned and taken away. A witness is frightened into silence.

Part 5

Alisa has run after the pirates and Kolya but has lost their track. The witness leads her in the wrong direction. The other children arrive to help searching, as Yulya has told them Alisa's secret. They worry that Kolya may be tortured in order to reveal where he keeps the myelophone. Fima believes that the device is still at Kolya's place and runs there in order to pick it up before the pirates arrive. The other children search the building where Alisa lost Kolya's track. In the abandoned house, the pirates start interrogating Kolya. Meanwhile Yulya reaches for a snack in her schoolbag and discovers the myelophone. The children use it to scan the remaining flats in the building. Alisa spots the witness and uses the myelophone on him. His thoughts tell that two men carried an uncoscious boy to the abandoned house. The children approach the house and are noticed by the pirates who also realise that Alisa carries the myelophone. As Kolya has fallen unconscious from the torture, the pirates assume his shape. One distracts most children, the other lures Alisa into the house. While she cares for Kolya, the pirate takes the myelophone. Howewer, the talent scout has also entered the house. When the pirate threatens her, she throws him out of the window. The other pirate takes the myelophone from him and tries to leave him behind in the 20th century. However, the access to the time machine is still blocked. The children rush in but one pirate fires his blaster, forcing the children to retreat. The door to the time machine opens and Polina enters in order to arrest the pirates. They fire on her as well but she is protected by a force field and paralyses them. Alisa says goodbye and tells the children what they are going to become in the future. While she enters the secret chamber and the door closes, we hear the song "Beautiful Tomorrow".

Cast

- Natalya Guseva as *Alisa Seleznyova*
- Aleksei Fomkin as *Kolya Gerasimov*
- Maryana Ionesyan as *Yulya Gribkova*
- Ilya Naumov as *Fima Korolyov*
- Vyacheslav Nevinny as *Veselchak U (lit. Jolly Man U)*
- Mikhail Kononov as *Krys (lit. Rat)*
- Georgi Burkov as *Alik Borisovich (doctor)*
- Yevgeni Gerasimov as *Robot Werther*
- Valentina Talyzina as *Mariya Pavlovna*
- Natalya Varley as *Marta Erastovna*
- Yelena Metyolkina as *Polina*
- Vladimir Nosik as *old man Pavel*
- Yuri Grigoryev as *Professor Seleznyov*
- Mariya Sternikova as *Shurochka*
- Andrei Gradov as *Ishutin*
- Inna Churkina as schoolgirl

Soundtrack

Wonderful Far-away (Prekrasnoe dalyoko)

The song was performed by the Grand Children chorus of Central Television and Gosteleradio USSR as the theme song for the film. The composer Ye.Krylatov, words Yu.Entin (Sample (youtube)). The song's popularity soon separated from the miniseries and it became iconic in its own right; it was widely performed by various choirs and sung in everyday life.

Cultural influence

- Many Soviet schoolboys fell in love with Alice played by Natalya Giseva, who had got a lot of letters from fans. This phenomenon was called as "Alicemania" (Алисомания) and had a large scale.
- Popular in early 2000s Russian dance group Гости из Будущего (Gosti iz Budushchego; Guests from the Future) got their name from the film title.

Source (edited): "http://en.wikipedia.org/wiki/Guest_from_the_Future"

Heart of a Dog (film)

Heart of a Dog (Russian: Собачье сердце, translit. *Sobachye serdtse*) is a black-and-white 1988 Soviet television film directed by Vladimir Bortko. It is based on Mikhail Bulgakov's novel *Heart of a Dog*.

Plot

The film is set in Moscow not long after the October Revolution. A well-off surgeon Filip Filippovich Preobrazhensky implants a pituitary gland and testicles of a recently deceased alcoholic and petty criminal Klim Chugunkin into a stray dog named Sharik. Sharik proceeds to become more and more human during the next days. After his transition to human is complete, it turns out that he inherited all the negative traits of the donor - bad manners, aggressiveness, use of profanity, heavy drinking. He picks for himself an absurd name Poligraf Poligrafovich Sharikov, starts working at the "Moscow Cleansing Department responsible for eliminating vagrant quadrupeds (cats, etc.)" and associating with revolutionaries, who plot to drive Preobrazhensky out of his big apartment. Eventually he turns the life in the professor's house into a nightmare, and the professor with his assistant are urged to reverse the procedure. Sharikov turns back into a dog. As Sharik he does not remember anything that happened and is left to life in the professor's apartment.

Cast

- Yevgeniy Yevstigneyev as *Professor Preobrazhensky*
- Boris Plotnikov as *Dr. Bormental*
- Vladimir Tolokonnikov as *Poly-*

graph Polygraphovich Sharikov
- Nina Ruslanova as *Darya*
- Roman Kartsev as *Schwonder*
- Olga Melikhova as *Zina*

Details

- This screen version of M. Bulgakov's novel is famous for its attention to the original text: practically nothing was deleted for adaptation. However, there are some differences between the novel and the film (in the novel Bormental didn't meet typist in the cinema and Pyotr Alexandrovich - an important official cured by Preobrazhensky - didn't look like Stalin as it was shown in the film). The episode in which Bormental presents Sharikov who plays balalaika didn't exist in the novel. However, the phrases of Bormental were taken from the diary of Bormental which was in the original novel.
- Some scenes (spiritualism, circus) were taken from early Bulgakov's short stories, not from the novel.
- One of the scientists who witness the transformation of Sharik into a human is called Professor Persikov. He is the protagonist of another Bulgakov's science-fiction novel *The Fatal Eggs*.

Source (edited): "http://en.wikipedia.org/wiki/Heart_of_a_Dog_(film)"

Ivan Vasilievich: Back to the Future

For the 1985 sci-fi film see Back to the Future

Ivan Vasilievich Changes Profession (Russian: Иван Васильевич меняет профессию, *Ivan Vasilyevich menyayet professiyu*) is a Soviet comedy film produced by Mosfilm in 1973. In the United States the film has sometimes been sold under the title **Ivan Vasilievich: Back to the Future**.

This film is based on a play by Mikhail Bulgakov and was one of the most attended movies in the Soviet Union in 1973 with more than 60 million tickets sold.

- Director: Leonid Gaidai
- Composer: Aleksandr Zatsepin
- Song lyrics: Leonid Derbenev
- Yuri Yakovlev (Ivan the Terrible / Ivan Vasilievich Bunsha)
- Leonid Kuravlev (George Miloslavsky)
- Aleksandr Demyanenko (Shurik)
- Natalia Selezneva (Zina)
- Natalia Krachkovskaya (Uliana Andreevna Bunsha)
- Vladimir Etush (Anton Semenovich Shpak)
- Mikhail Pugovkin (director Yakin)
- Natalia Kustinskaya (Yakin's mistress)
- Sergey Filippov (Swedish ambassador)
- Saveliy Kramarov (Feofan the clerk)
- Edward Bredun (black market seller)
- Natalia Gurzo (Shpak's dental assistant)
- Nina Maslova (Tsaritza Marfa)
- Viktor Uralsky (Police sergeant-major)
- Leonid Gaidai (Yakin's light assistant)

Plot summary

The movie begins in 1973 Moscow, where Engineer Shurik (Aleksandr Demyanenko) is working on a time machine in his apartment. By accident, he sends Ivan Vasilevich Bunsha (Yuri Yakovlev), superintendent of his apartment building, and George Miloslavsky (Leonid Kuravlev), a small-time burglar, back into the time of Ivan IV. The pair is forced to disguise themselves, with Bunsha dressing up as Ivan IV and Miloslavsky as a knyaz of the same name (who everybody thought was executed by the tsar). At the same time, the real Ivan IV (also played by Yuri Yakovlev) is sent by the same machine into Shurik's apartment, he has to deal with modern-day life while Shurik tries to fix the machine so that everyone can be brought back to their proper place in time. As the police (tipped off by a neighbor who was burgled by Miloslavsky) close in on Shurik, who is frantically trying to repair the machine, the cover of Bunsha and Miloslavsky is blown and they have to fight off the Streltsy, who have figured out that Bunsha is not the real Tsar. The movie ends with Bunsha, Miloslavsky, and Ivan IV all transported back to their proper places, although the entire thing is revealed to be a dream by Shurik. Or was it?

Production

VHS film cover

- The beginning and ending scenes are in black-and-white, while the rest of the movie is in color. This was done to show the contrast between reality and dream (respectively), and perhaps as a tongue-in-cheek homage to *The Wizard of Oz*.
- In the scene where Bunsha meets with the Swedish ambassador, the first thing he says is "Hitler kaputt!" It's one of the most recognizable phrases on German for majority of Russians. However, the original script had him say "Peace - friendship!", but the Soviet censors thought it inappropriate. The resulting change ended up being more humorous.

- Not only Bunsha is mistaken for the tsar, but Ivan IV has to deal with Bunsha's wife who believes him to be her husband.
- Bunsha's wife's hair keeps changing every scene. This is revealed to be because she wears wigs.
- There are several events which could have had dire consequences to the timeline had the whole thing not turned out to be a dream:
  - Ivan IV sees a painting in Shurik's apartment - *Ivan the Terrible killing his son* by Ilya Repin, but the event itself is only supposed to happen later in his life. It is clear, though, that he does not recognize the person (himself) in the painting.
  - Before stealing the Swedish ambassador's medallion, Miloslavsky distracts him by giving him a novelty ballpoint pen centuries before they are invented.
  - Ivan IV at one point is listening to the "Hare's Song" on the tape-player, a song from Gaidai's *The Diamond Arm*.
  - Ivan IV finding out that Boris Godunov would succeed him by hearing about Pushkin's play.
- The movie is an inspiration for an Indian movie starring Paresh Rawal called fun2sh.

Locations

Film locations
- Moscow, Russian Federation
- Rostov, Russian Federation

Shooting locations
- Mosfilm Studios
- Rostov Kremlin, Rostov
- Streets of Moscow

Deviations from the original play

The original play was written by Bulgakov in 1935 (albeit not published until 1965) and, therefore, used a setting typical to the 1930s. The film, released in 1973, made changes to the setting to make it contemporary. For instance, Shpak's phonograph was replaced in the film with a tape recorder, and the time machine was envisioned as using more advanced technology such as transistors. In addition, inventor Timofeyev is inspired to travel to Ivan IV's era after seeing a film about it on television, as opposed to listening to the play *Pskovityanka* on the radio.

There were other deviations, not related to changes designed to modernize the setting. While the inventor's surname Timofeyev was retained, he was called Nikolai (nicknamed "Koka" by his wife Zinaida), while in the film, his name is Alexander (called "Shurik" informally). He is presumably an older version of the protagonist of two previous Leonid Gaidai films: *Operation Y and Other Shurik's Adventures* and *Kidnapping, Caucasian Style*, played by the same actor, Aleksandr Demyanenko; this connection, though, is not stated outright and neither of these earlier films are referenced.

In addition, the reason for the time machine malfunction was changed. In the original play, Bunsha and Miloslavsky knowingly disable the machine to seal the gateway between the two time periods, but are dragged into the past, along with the key to the machine, forcing Timofeyev to make a replacement key. In the film, the time machine is accidentally damaged by a halberd, and Timofeyev has to search for some transistors to repair it.

Finally, while the "all just a dream" ending is present in both the play and the film, the play ends on a revelation that Shpak's apartment has been robbed in reality, not only in the dream. This twist is absent in the film.

In the play, Ivan Vasilievich Bunsha is the son of a nobleman, something which, as a conscientious Soviet bureaucrat, he tries to hide. This isn't mentioned in the film.

Despite the aforementioned inconsistencies, the film can be considered a fairly faithful and accurate adaptation.
Source (edited): "http://en.wikipedia.org/wiki/Ivan_Vasilievich:_Back_to_the_Future"

Kin-dza-dza!

Kin-dza-dza! (Russian: Кин-дза-дза!, translit. *Kin-dzah-dzah!*) is a 1986 Soviet comedy-science fiction film released by the Mosfilm studio and directed by Georgi Daneliya, with a story by Georgi Daneliya and Revaz Gabriadze. The movie was filmed in color, consists of two parts and runs for 135 minutes in total.

The film is a dark and grotesque parody of human society and may be described as a dystopia. It depicts a desert planet, depleted of its resources, home to an impoverished dog-eat-dog society with extreme inequality and oppression. It is a cult film, especially in post-Soviet countries, and its humorous dialogue is frequently quoted.

Plot

The story takes place on the desert planet "Pluke" in the "Kin-dza-dza" galaxy, where two Soviet humans previously unknown to each other ("Uncle Vova", a gruff construction foreman from Moscow Vladimir Moshkov, and "The Fiddler", a student from Georgia Gedevan Aleksidze) are stranded due to an accidental encounter with an alien teleportation device. The movie describes their long quest to find a way back home.

The natives of the planet appear human, with deceptively primitive-looking technology and a barbaric culture, which satirically resembles that of humans. They are telepathic; the only spoken words normally used in their culture are "ku" (koo) and "kyu" (kew), the latter being a swear word. However, the Plukanians are able to quickly adapt to understand and speak Russian (and Georgian too). The society of Pluke is divided into two categories: *Chatlanians* and *Patsaks*. Chatlanians are privileged, and a system of rituals must be followed by the Patsaks to show flattery. The basis of their difference is unexplainable (a source of a humorous episode), and for all practical matters they are distinguished with aid of a small handheld device (*visator*). It is also noted that the social differences between Patsaks and Chatlanians aren't constant: Pluke being a Chatlanian planet, they are privileged there; but there are Patsak planets where Patsaks hold the upper hand and Chatlanians are subservient. Wef and Bi switch their social roles immediately and without any problems when visiting one such planet.

The only group empowered to use weapons (*"tranklucators"*) and enforce their will is the *ecilops* ("police" spelled backwards). The nominal leader of the Plukanian society is named *PG*; everybody makes their best to display fervent worship to him and disrespect is severely punished; but, when encountered in person, PG appears harmless and dumb. The fuel of Pluke is called *lutz* and is made from water. All naturally present water has apparently been processed into lutz, so drinking water is a valuable commodity (in fact, it can only be made from lutz).

A good deal of the plot is based on the fact that ordinary wooden matchsticks (*ketse*) (or, rather, the chemicals of the match head) are considered to be extremely valuable on Pluke.

A Concise Dictionary of The Plukanian Language

- Ketse (pronounced "keh-tseh") — matches (or, rather, the chemicals ordinarily used on Earth for match heads)
- Chatle — a currency unit
- Tsak — a small bell worn on the nose to indicate the low social status of the wearer
- Tentura and Antitentura — two opposite parts of the Universe. Some planets and galaxies exist in Tentura and some (including Earth) in Antitentura.
- Pepelatz — an interplanetary spacecraft (from the Georgian word "pepela" for butterfly)
- Tsapa — a component for different machines. A *big tsapa* is a very important component for the pepelatz. A *small tsapa* is a component for the gravitsapa; without the small tsapa, a gravitsapa will not work. Tsapa is similar to a very rusty screwnut
- Gravitsapa — a component for the pepelatz which allows intergalactic travel (from 'gravity' + 'tsapa')
- Tranklucator — a weapon
- Visator — compact device, detects difference between Patsaks and Chatlanians.
- Kappa — a button or lever
- Lutz (pronounced loots) — the fuel used by the pepelatz, it is made of water
- Ecilop — a policeman ("police" spoken backwards)
- Ecikh — a box for prisoners; also the inprisonment in such box (as a penalty); also *the Ecikh* is a jail with many such boxes ("Ecikh" is from the Georgian word "tsikhe" for prison). *Ecikh with nails* is extremely hard punishment.
- Kyu (pronounced kyew) — a socially acceptable curse (meaning 'shit')
- Koo — All other words

Video

The movie has been released on DVD in Russia but has gained virtually no notice elsewhere, with the exception of Japan. This is largely due to the fact that there was no official release of the movie with English subtitles for a long time. This has led many people to download copies of the movie from popular peer-to-peer services: most English-speaking people who have seen the movie have seen a fansub or watched it with a friend who can translate.

There are currently no plans to release the DVD in Europe or North America.

In the year 2005 RUSCICO (Russian Cinema Council) released a version with Russian original sound and with English and French dubbing, It has also subtitles in English and other languages.

Cast (in order of appearance)

- Stanislav Lyubshin as *Vladimir Nikolayevich Mashkov (Uncle Vova)*
- Galina Daneliya-Yurkova as *Lyudmila (Lucya), the Mashkov's wife*
- Levan Gabriadze as *Gedevan Alexandrovich Alexidze (The Fiddler)*
- Anatoli Serenko as *the Barefoot Wanderer from Uzm*
- Yury Yakovlev as *Bi the Patsak, a wandering singer*
- Yevgeny Leonov as *Wef the Chatlanian, a wandering singer*
- ? as *one-handed smuggler with a mini tranklucator*
- ? (Tatyana Proshina?) as *female smuggler with a mini tranklucator, girlfriend of the gang leader*
- Alexander Litovkin as *the gang leader*
- Valentin Bukin as *black-moustached ecilop in an egg-shaped pepelatz, demonstrating how a tranklucator works*
- Irina Shmelyova as *Tsan, the cart driver* (tachanka-driving woman, a wandering singer and dancer)
- Lev Perfilov as *Kyrr, the dissident Chatlanian with a tranklucator*
- Nina Ruslanova as *Galina Borisovna, the vice-dean*
- Yuri Voronkov as *bearded Chatlanian, leader of the "Children of the Sun" sect (later seen in the subway train, pretending to be a Patsak)*
- ? as *sinister man in a grey cap (leader's helper?)*
- ? as *acrobat sectarian Patsak girl*
- Olesya Ivanova as *cage-banging white sectarian woman*
- Lyudmila Solodenko as *sand-throwing black sectarian girl*
- Vitali Leonov as *Shorty (from the sect)*
- ? as *sectarian in a red cap*
- ? as *Longshanks (from the sect)*
- ? as *tall sectarian woman in bridges*
- ? as *sectarian woman in yellow shirt*
- ? as *sectarian watcher on the big wheel ('Danger, ECILOP!!!')*
- Nikolai Garo as *Lord PG*
- Igor Bogolyubov as *Lord PG's Personal Patsak*
- Victor Marenkov as *Patsak, wearing*

- a coil pipe for a mask and working as watchman
- Aleksandr Gorbachyov as *grey-moustached elderly ecilop in an egg-shaped pepelatz, who will want "40 chatles" and "immediately press the kappa" in a scene later*
- Yelena Mashkova-Sulakadze as *watchman's wife (redheaded Patsak woman in the trapdoor)*
- Gennady B.Ivanov as *black ecilop, guarding the underground communications*
- Aleksandra Dorokhina as *colossal Chatlanian woman, working as attendant in the subway station*
- ? as *Patsak in the subway*
- ? (Tatyana Perfilyeva?) as *old Patsak woman "I like Lord PG so much!"*
- ? as *old ecilop giving permission to proceed*
- ? as *young ecilop, guarding the water factory*
- Victor Makhmutov as *the red-headed Chatlanian*
- ? (Valeri Svetlov?) as *muzzled little man*
- ? as *fat Patsak woman with a purple purse on her backside*
- Vladimir Fyodorov as *Mr. Yellow Pants*
- ? as *Mr. Yellow Pants' bodyguard*
- Yelena Antonova as *Mr. Yellow Pants' girlfriend*
- ? as *Mr. Yellow Pants' wife*
- Tatyana Novitskaya as *an employee in the planetarium*
- Yuri Naumtsev as *the judge*
- Gennady Yalovich as *secret agent*
- Veronica Izotova as *the gang leader's female Chatlanian slave, wearing a collar*
- Vladimir Razumovsky as *ecilop with muzzles*
- Nina Ter-Osipian as *Lord PG's noble mother*
- Harri Schweitz as *Lord PG's 1st bodyguard (bearded fatman)*
- Valentin Golubenko as *Lord PG's 2nd bodyguard (long-nosed powerman)*
- Oleg Matveyev as *Lord PG's 3rd bodyguard (young man wearing gloves)*
- ? as *jailer in the Ecikh*
- Olga Mashnaya as *Dekont (from the planet Alpha)*
- Georgi Daneliya as *Abradox (from the planet Alpha)*
- Varvara Vladimirova as *young Alphian mother*
- Anya Andriyanova as *little blonde Alphian girl*
- ? as *young Alphian man*
- ? as *young Alphian girl*
- Rene Khobua was not in the cast, but present in subtitles

Bi, Wef and their pepelatz. Graffiti. Kharkov, 2008

Animated version

An animated version of the same story, named *Kin-dza-dza-dza!*, is being made in Russia, and is planned for release in Summer 2011. This version will be targeted more at children and the international audience. Work began on February 12, 2005, and it has a budget of three million rubles. The finished film is expected to be 100 minutes long.
Source (edited): "http://en.wikipedia.org/wiki/Kin-dza-dza!"

Kosmicheskiy reys

Kosmicheskiy reys: Fantasticheskaya novella (known in English as ***Cosmic Voyage*** and ***The Space Voyage***) is a 1936 Soviet science fiction produced by Mosfilm.

Plot

In the year 1946, the Soviet space program is undergoing turmoil. Professor Sedikh, who is planning to lead the first manned exploration to the moon, is denounced by his rival Professor Karin as being too old and too mentally unstable for the mission. Professor Sedikh, aided by his assistant Marina and a youth named Andryusha, disregard Prof. Karin's authority and make a successful landing on the moon. Although a few problems occur at the moon, including the discovery of a damaged oxygen tank and Professor Sedikh's becoming trapped under a fallen boulder, the expedition is a success and the cosmonauts return to Moscow.

Cast

- Sergei Komarov...Pavel Ivanovich Sedikh
- K. Moskalenko...Professor Marina
- Vassili Gaponenko...Andryusha Orlov
- Nikolai Feoktistov...Capt. Viktor Orlov
- Vasili Kovrigin...Professor Karin

Production

Kosmicheskiy reys: Fantasticheskaya novella was initially conceived in 1924 by Russian filmmaker Vasili Zhuravlov, but it was not pursued for production until 1932, when Komsomol (the Communist Union of Youth) recommended the creation of film that would spur an interest in space studies. Zhuravlov consulted with Konstantin Tsiolkovsky, the noted aeronautical theorist and rocket science engineer, on the screenplay. Tsiolkovsky died shortly after the film was completed.

Two spaceships in the film were named after the Soviet leaders Josef Stalin and Kliment Voroshilov. The film's cosmonauts enter liquid-filled chambers to buffer the impact of takeoff and landing, and they communicate their landing to the Earth by spelling out "CCCP" (the Russian-language acronym for "USSR") with reflective substances spread across the lunar surface.

Kosmicheskiy reys: Fantasticheskaya novella was shot as a silent film and only had a brief release in early 1936 before being removed from circulation by Soviet censors, who felt that an animated sequence of cosmonauts hopping across the gravity-free lunar surface was antithetical to the spirit of "socialist realism." It was not widely seen again until the 1980s.

Source (edited): "http://en.wikipedia.org/wiki/Kosmicheskiy_reys"

Moscow-Cassiopeia

Moscow-Cassiopeia (Russian: Москва — Кассиопея) is a Soviet 1973 film directed by Richard Viktorov based on a script by Isai Kuznetsov and Avenir Zak. Followed by Otroki vo vselennoy (second part, 1974). Runtime - 85 min.

Plot summary

From the depths of the universe and the Earth could hear the radio signals of intelligent beings from the planet of the star systems Shedar (Alpha Cassiopeia constellation). The project, proposed by the young inventor Vitya Sereda, should allow the spaceship to reach the planet Earth - but the flight will last for decades, so the crew of the spaceship "Dawn " (Starship relativistic nuclear annihilation), recruited from students.

All carefully thought out, but the secret to get to the spaceship mischief and Fibber Fyodor Lobanov unwittingly arranges so that the ship exceeds the speed of light, is the target for 27 years ahead of schedule.

Cast

- Innokenti Smoktunovsky as *I.O.O.* (Special Service Executive)
- Vasili Merkuryev as *academician Blagovidov*
- Lev Durov as *academician Filatov*
- Yuri Medvedev as *academician Ogon-Duganovsky*
- Pyotr Merkuryev as *academician Kurochkin*

Space ship *DAWN* crew

- Mikhail Yershov as *Sereda*
- Aleksandr Grigoryev as *Kozelkov*
- Vladimir Savin as *Kopanygin*
- Vladimir Basov Jr. as *Lobanov*
- Olga Bityukova as *Kuteishchikova*
- Nadezhda Ovcharova as *Sorokina*
- Irina Popova as *Panfyorova*

Other cast

- Anatoli Adoskin
- Natalya Fateyeva
- Nikolai Figurovsky
- Artyom Karapetyan
- Valentina Kutsenko
- Sergei Radchenko
- Raisa Ryazanova
- Nadezhda Semyontsova
- Natalya Strizhenova
- Anna Viktorova
- Nikolai Viktorov
- Mikhail Yanushkevich
- V. Zolotaryov

Trivia

- ZARYa stands for Spaceship (Zvezdolet) Annihilation Relativistical Nuclear (Yaderniy)

Awards

- Premio for the Best Film for Kids of the All-Union Cinema Festival, Baku, 1974
- Special Premio of the International Cinema Festival of Science Fiction Films, Triest, 1975
- Special Prize of the International Cinema Festival (in the Children films category), Moscow, 1975
- *Platero* Prize of the International Cinema Festival as the film for the Kids and Youth, Gijón, 1975.
- Diploma of the Moscow Technical Contest of the Films, UNIATEK congress, Moscow, 1976
- State Premio of RSFSR in the honour of Vasilyiev Brothers, 1977.

Source (edited): "http://en.wikipedia.org/wiki/Moscow-Cassiopeia"

Mysterious Island (1941 film)

Mysterious Island, or *Tainstvennyy ostrov* in Russian, is a USSR film adaptation of the 1874 novel by Jules Verne, *The Mysterious Island* (*L'Île mystérieuse*). The story is a follow-up to *Twenty Thousand Leagues Under the Sea*.

Plot summary

During the siege of Richmond, Virginia, in the American Civil War, five northern prisoners of war decide to escape in a rather unusual way – by hijacking a balloon.

The group eventually crash-lands on a cliff-bound, volcanic, unknown (and fictitious) island, located in the South Pacific. They name it "Lincoln Island" in honour of American President Abraham Lincoln. With the knowledge of the brilliant engineer, the five are able to sustain themselves on the island, producing fire, pottery, bricks, nitroglycerine, iron, a simple electric telegraph, and even a seaworthy ship. They also manage to find their geographical location.

The mystery of the island seems to come from periodic and inexplicable *deus ex machinas*: the unexplainable survival of Smith from his fall from the balloon, the mysterious rescue of his dog Top from a wild manatee, a box full of equipment (guns and ammunition, tools, etc...), the finding of a message in the sea calling for help, and so on.

A crew of pirates arrives at the Lincoln Island to use it as their hideout. After some fighting with the heroes, the pirate ship is mysteriously destroyed by an explosion, and the pirates themselves are found dead, apparently in combat, but with no visible wounds.

The secret of the island is revealed

when it turns out to be Captain Nemo's hideout, and home harbour of the *Nautilus*. Captain Nemo had been the savior of the heroes, providing them with equipment, sending a message about a fellow castaway, torpedoing the pirate ship and killing the pirates with an electric gun.

Cast

A. Andriyenko-Zemskov ... Pencroft
Yuri Grammatikati ... Herbert
Pavel Kiyansky .... Gideon Spillett
Nikolai Komissarov ... Captain Nemo
I. Kozlov ... Ayrton
Alexei Krasnopolsky .... Capt. Cyrus Harding (Smith)
R. Ross .... Neb
Andrei Sova .... Jupe

Crew

B. M. Chelintsev and Eduard Pentslin (directors) M. Kalinin, Boris Shelontsev, and Jules Verne (writers)
Source (edited): "http://en.wikipedia.org/wiki/Mysterious_Island_(1941_film)"

New Adventures of a Yankee in King Arthur's Court

New Adventures of a Yankee in King Arthur's Court. Fantasy over Mark Twain's theme (Russian: Новые приключения янки при дворе короля Артура. Фантазии на тему Марка Твена) is a 1988 Soviet adventure film directed by Viktor Hres and based on American author Mark Twain's *A Connecticut Yankee in King Arthur's Court*. The screenplay was written by Mikhail Roshchin, and the film was produced by Dovzhenko Film Studio.

Plot summary

A plane crashes in the time of King Arthur. The surviving pilot tries to accommodate to this strange new world.

Cast

- Sergei Koltakov as Hank Morgan
- Albert Filozov as King Arthur / Merlin
- Yelena Finogeyeva as Queen Ginevra
- Aleksandr Kaidanovsky as Sir Lancelot
- Anastasiya Vertinskaya as Morgan Le Fay
- Yevgeniy Yevstigneyev as Archbishop
- Yevdokiya Germanova as Cindy
- Vladimir Soshalsky as Sagramor
- Vladimir Kashpur
- Mark Gres as Mordraig
- Anatoli Stolbov
- Mariya Kapnist
- Francisco Rodríguez
- José Vega
- Valeri Gribov

Source (edited): "http://en.wikipedia.org/wiki/New_Adventures_of_a_Yankee_in_King_Arthur%27s_Court"

Per Aspera Ad Astra (film)

Per Aspera Ad Astra (Russian: Через тернии к звёздам, USA screen name - *Through the Thorns to the Stars*; *Humanoid Woman*) is a 1981 Soviet film directed by Richard Viktorov based on a novel by Kir Bulychyov.

On December 27, 2001 a new restored version directed by Nikolai Viktorov, the son of the original film's director, was released as the 20th anniversary edition . The film featured revised special effects by the Paradox company, an all-new soundtrack in Dolby Digital and the film length had shrunk by 25 min (to speed up the dynamics of the plot; but also some episodes with Soviet ideological context were cut).

An English-dubbed version of the film (under the title *Humanoid Woman*) was featured on an early episode of *Mystery Science Theater 3000*.

Plot summary

XXIII century. A reconnaissance starship discovers a dead alien spaceship of unknown origin in deep space. The crew are found to be humanoid bodies, made by an advanced cloning process. One humanoid woman appears to be alive but has memory loss and is brought back to Earth. Scientist Sergei Lebedev settles her in his own house and names her Niya.

Some time later, Niya finds out that she has supernatural abilities. Prof. Ivanova finds a special neurocenter in her brain which can be used to control the humanoid clones. Niya suddenly remembers her home planet Dessa, where businessmen eager for easy money destroy nature.

A rescue mission with Niya on board is sent to her home planet. When she arrives there, her brain falls under the control of the neurowaves of local monopolist Turanchoks, who is trying to make the Earth expedition fail.

However, Niya is strong enough to resist the control and saves her civilization from an imminent catastrophe.

Cast

- Yelena Metyolkina as *Niya*
- Uldis Lieldidz as *Cadet Stepan Lebedev*
- Vadim Ledogorovas *Sergei Lebedev*
- Yelena Fadeyeva as *Maria Pavlovna*
- Vatslav Dvorzhetsky as *Petr Petrovich*
- Nadezhda Semyontsova as *Professor Nadezhda Ivanova*
- Aleksandr Lazarev as *Professor Klimov*
- Aleksandr Mikhajlov as *Dreier*
- Boris Shcherbakov as *Navigator Kolotin*
- Igor Ledogorov as *Ambassador Rakan*
- Igor Yasulovich as *Torki*
- Gleb Strizhenov as *Glan*
- Vladimir Fyodorov as *Turanchoks*
- Yevgeni Karelskikh

Source (edited): "http://en.wikipedia.org/wiki/Per_Aspera_Ad_Astra_(film)"

Polygon (film)

Polygon (Russian: Полигон, *The Shooting range*) is a 1977 Soviet animation science fiction short film.

Plot summary

The plot is based on an anti-war military science fiction story by Sever Gansovsky.

In the not-too-distant future a scientist from a military great power wants revenge for his son (who was a soldier KIA during war) and thus invents a weapon capable of ending the conflict - an automated mind-reading tank that detects and reacts to human feelings of hostility and fear. After his revenge successfully takes place (as the tank destroys a number of generals responsible for the loss of his son) he himself falls victim to his own creation.

The film has an open ending.

Voice cast

- Vsevolod Yakut
- Oleg Mokshantsev
- Alexander Beliavsky
- Anatoly Kuznetsov
- S. Martynov

Production Information

Polygon was directed by Anatoly Petrov (b. 1937) and it was based on a screenplay by Sever Gansovsky (edited by Arcady Snessarev). The short film was produced by Lubov' Butyrina and released by Soyuzmultfilm studio. It featured the artwork of artists Elena Karavaeva, Olga Bogolubova, I. Kulakova, Elena Bogolubova and N. Ivancheva. The art director was Galina Barinova.

The animator was Vladimir Zarubin under the supervision of Anatoly Petrov. It was filmed by cameraman Michael Druyan and the sound effects and music were created by Vladimir Kutuzov.

Animation Technique

A screen shot of the short showing a character similar to Ringo Starr.

The film was drawn in an unusual animation technique called *photographica* that consists of two celluloid layers for each character with special color schemes and with one of the layers out of focus to imitate the three-dimensional space rendering. The animation then actively moves the virtual camera to change perspective dynamically for each scene and give a sense of realism, without the use of any CGI methods (which weren't available at the time).

The characters in this animated film were designed with faces very similar to those of several famous movie actors and celebrities of the time, including Ringo Starr, Jean Gabin, Paul Newman, Yul Brynner and Mel Ferrer (The scientist) among others.

Awards

The film won the following awards:
- First Prize at the Yerevan Film Festival (USSR, 1978).
- Official Selection at the Oberhausen Film Festival (Germany, 1979).

Source (edited): "http://en.wikipedia.org/wiki/Polygon_(film)"

Solaris (1968 film)

Solaris (Russian: Солярис) is a 1968 TV film based on the 1961 novel *Solaris* by Stanisław Lem. It was written by N. Kemarsky, directed by Boris Nirenburg and was a Central Television production.

Cast

- A. Pilius as Hari
- Vasily Lanovoy as Chris Kelvin
- Vladimir Etush as Dr. Snaut
- V. Zozulin as Dr. Sartorius

Source (edited): "http://en.wikipedia.org/wiki/Solaris_(1968_film)"

Solaris (1972 film)

Solaris (Russian: «Солярис», tr. *Solyaris*) is a 1972 film adaptation of the novel *Solaris* (1961), directed by Andrei Tarkovsky. The film is a meditative psychological drama occurring mostly aboard a space station orbiting the fictional planet Solaris. The scientific mission has stalled, because the scientist crew have fallen to emotional crises. Psychologist Kris Kelvin travels to the Solaris space station, to learn and evaluate the situation—yet soon hallucinates like the others.

The Polish science fiction novel by Stanisław Lem is about the ultimate inadequacy of communication between human and non-human species. Tarkovsky's adaptation is a "drama of grief and partial recovery" concentrated upon the thoughts and the consciences of the cosmonaut scientists studying an extra-terrestrial (alien) life. The psychologically complex and slow narrative of *Solaris* has been contrasted to kinetic Western science fiction films, which rely upon fast narrative pace and special effects to communicate character psychology and an imagined future. The ideas which Tarkovsky tried to express in this film are further developed in *Stalker* (1979).

The critically successful *Solaris* features Natalya Bondarchuk (Hari), Donatas Banionis (Kris Kelvin), Jüri Järvet (Dr Snaut), Vladislav Dvorzhetsky (Henri Burton), Nikolai Grinko (Kris Kelvin's Father), Olga Barnet (Kris Kelvin's Mother), Anatoli Solonitsyn (Dr Sartorius), and Sos Sargsyan (Dr Gibarian); the music score is by Eduard Artemyev. At the 1972 Cannes Film Festival, it won the Grand Prix Spécial du Jury, the FIPRESCI prize and was nominated for the Palme d'Or.

Plot summary

Psychologist Kris Kelvin (Donatas Banionis) spends his last day on Earth reflecting on his life while walking by a lake near his childhood home where his elderly father still lives. Kelvin is about to embark on an interstellar journey to a space station orbiting the remote oceanic planet Solaris. After decades of study, the scientific mission at the space station has barely progressed in its goal of understanding the planet. To make matters worse, most of the crew has succumbed to a series of emotional crises. Kelvin is dispatched to evaluate the situation aboard ship and determine whether the venture should continue.

Henri Burton (Vladislav Dvorzhetsky), a former space pilot, visits Kelvin. They watch film footage of Burton's own testimony years before of seeing an over-sized child on the ocean surface of Solaris while searching for two lost scientists. However, the cameras of his craft recorded only clouds and the flat ocean surface; Burton's report was dismissed as hallucinations. After failing to convince Kelvin of the truth of his experience, Burton leaves angrily only to later call Kelvin. He explains that he met the child of a scientist lost in that mission, and the child was reminiscent of the one he saw on Solaris.

Before departing Earth for Solaris, Kelvin destroys most of his personal mementos in a bonfire, noting the volume of keepsakes he has accumulated. In Kelvin's last conversation with his father (Nikolai Grinko), they realize that the father will not live to see Kelvin return. Although he readily accepted the mission, it is a choice that weighs heavily upon Kelvin's conscience.

Upon arrival at the Solaris space station, none of the three remaining scientists meet Kelvin, who finds the disarrayed space station dangerously neglected. He soon learns that his friend among the scientists, Dr. Gibarian (Sos Sargsyan), has mysteriously died. The two surviving crewmen are unhelpful, and give contradicting and confusing information. Shortly thereafter, Dr. Snaut (Jüri Järvet) warns Kelvin not to overreact if he sees anything "unusual" on board the station. However, Kelvin soon glimpses other people aboard the station. While Kelvin sends news of the chaos on board the station, the oceans of Solaris begin swirling on the planet's surface.

Waking exhausted from a restless sleep, Kelvin finds a woman with him in his quarters despite the barricaded door. To his surprise, it is Hari (Natalya Bondarchuk), his late wife who committed suicide some years before. However, she is mysteriously unaware of having committed suicide on Earth, and she is equally puzzled as to her presence in Kelvin's quarters. Grasping that she is a psychological construct brought on by the mysterious effects of Solaris, he lures her to a spacecraft and launches the illusion of his wife into outer space. In his haste to be rid of her, he is burned by the rocket's blast. Dr. Snaut tends his burns and explains that the "visitors" began appearing after the scientists attracted the attention of Solaris, seemingly a sentient entity.

That evening, Hari reappears in his quarters. This time calm, Kelvin embraces Hari through the night. Later, Kelvin causes her to panic when she discovers the clothes of the first apparition and tries to leave the room. She beats her way through the room's metal door, severely cutting herself. Kelvin carries her back to his bed, where her injuries heal before his eyes. Dr. Sartorius (Anatoli Solonitsyn) calls for a meeting, and Kelvin introduces Hari as his wife, insisting they treat her respectfully. In their symposium, the scientists begin to understand that Solaris created Hari from Kelvin's memories of his dead wife. The Hari present among them, though not human, thinks and feels as though she were. Sartorius theorizes the visitors are composed of neutrinos and that it might be possible to destroy them.

Kelvin shows Hari films of himself and his parents when he was a boy and, later, of his wife. While she is asleep, Snaut proposes beaming Kelvin's brain-wave patterns at Solaris in hopes that it will understand them and stop the disturbing apparitions as communication. However, Sartorius suggests a radical attack of heavy radiation bombardment. In time, Hari becomes independent and is able to exist beyond Kelvin's sight. She learns from Sartorius that the original Hari had committed suicide ten years earlier, and Kelvin is forced to tell her the entire story. Distressed, Hari kills herself again by drinking liquid oxygen, only to painfully, spasmodically resurrect a few minutes later. On the surface of Solaris, the ocean is moving even faster.

In a fevered sleep, Kelvin dreams of his mother and of many Haris walking about his quarters. When he awakens, Hari is gone, and Snaut reads him the good-bye note she wrote him. The note indicates that Hari asked the scientists to kill her. Snaut tells Kelvin that since they broadcast Kelvin's brainwaves at Solaris, the visitors stopped appearing, and islands began forming on the planet's surface. Kelvin debates whether or not to return to Earth or to descend to Solaris in hope of reconnecting with everything he has loved and lost.

Again at the shore of the frozen lake, Kelvin finds himself at his father's house. His dog runs to him, and he happily walks towards it. He realizes something is wrong when he sees water is falling *inside* the house but is unnoticed by his father, who appears in the house. Father and son embrace on the front step of the lakeside house, on an island in the middle of an ocean on Solaris.

Production

Writing

In 1968, the director Andrei Tarkovsky had two motives for cinematically adapting the Polish science fiction novel *Solaris* (1961), Stanisław Lem: firstly, he admired Lem's work. Secondly, he needed work and money, because his previous film, *Andrei Rublev* (1966) had gone unreleased, and his screenplay, *A White, White Day,* had been rejected, yet it later was realised as *The Mirror* (1975). A film of a novel by Stanisław Lem, a popular and critically respected writer in the USSR, was a logical commercial and artistic choice. Tarkovsky and Lem collaborated, and remained in communication about the cinematic adaptation of the novel *Solaris*. With Fridrikh Gorenshtein, Tarkovsky co-wrote the first screenplay in the summer of 1969, two-thirds concerned the Earth marital history of Kris and Hari; Lem and the Mosfilm committee disliked it. The final screenplay, yielding the shooting script, has little action on Earth, and Kelvin's marriage to his second wife, Maria, was deleted from the story.

Solaris: A detail of *The Hunters in the Snow* (1565), by Pieter Bruegel, a thematic reference.

In the literary *Solaris*, Stanisław Lem describes human science's inability to handle an alien life form, because extraterrestrial life is beyond human understanding; in the cinematic *Solaris*, Tarkovsky concentrates upon Kelvin's feelings for his wife, Hari, and the impact of outer space exploration upon the human condition. Dr. Gibarian's monologue [from the novel's sixth chapter] is the highlight of the final library scene, wherein Snaut says, "We don't need other worlds. We need mirrors". Unlike the novel, which begins with psychologist Kris Kelvin's spaceflight, and occurs entirely on Solaris, the film shows Kelvin's visit to the house of his parents, in the country, before leaving Earth for Solaris; the contrast establishes the worlds in which he lives — warm Earth versus a cold space station orbiting the planet Solaris — showing and questioning space exploration's impact upon the human psyche.

The *Solaris* soundtrack features the chorale prelude for organ, *Ich ruf' zu dir, Herr Jesu Christ* (BWV 639), by Johann Sebastian Bach, and an electronic score by Eduard Artemyev, and the set design features paintings by the Old Masters. The interior of the space station is decorated with full reproductions of the 1565 painting cycle of *The Months* (*The Hunters in the Snow*, *The Gloomy Day*, *The Hay Harvest*, *The Harvesters*, and *The Return of the Herd*), by Pieter Bruegel the Elder, and details of *Landscape with the Fall of Icarus* and *The Hunters in the Snow* (1565). The scenes of Kelvin kneeling before his father, and the father embracing him allude to *The Return of the Prodigal Son* (1669), by Rembrandt. The references and allusions are Tarkovsky's efforts to give the young art of cinema an historic perspective of centuries, to evoke the viewer's feeling that cinema is a mature art.

The cast

Initially, Tarkovsky wanted his ex-wife, Irma Raush, as "Hari", however, after meeting Swedish actress Bibi Andersson in June 1970, he considered her for the role. Wishing to work with Tarkovsky, Andersson accepted her salary in rubles. In the end, Natalya Bondarchuk was cast as "Hari". Tarkovsky had met her when they were students at the State Institute of Cinematography; she had introduced *Solaris*, by Stanisław Lem, to him. Tarkovsky auditioned her in 1970, but did not cast her for being too young, and, instead, recommended her to director Larisa Shepitko, who cast her in *You and I*. Half-a-year later, Tarkovsky saw that film, and decided to cast Natalya Bondarchuk as "Hari".

Tarkovsky cast Lithuanian actor Donatas Banionis as "Kris Kelvin", the Estonian actor Jüri Järvet as "Dr. Snaut", the Russian actor Anatoly Solonitsyn as "Dr. Sartorius", the Ukrainian actor Nikolai Grinko as "Kelvin's Father", and Olga Barnet as "Kelvin's Mother". Earlier, the director had worked with Solonitsyn, who had played *Andrei Rublev* (1966), and with Nikolai Grinko, who appeared in *Andrei Rublev* and *Ivan's Childhood* (1962). Tarkovsky thought Solonitsyn and Grinko, would need extra directorial assistance. After filming was almost completed, Tarkovsky rated actors and performances, so: Bondarchuk, Järvet, Solonitsyn, Banionis, Dvorzhetsky, and Grinko; yet wrote in his diary that "Natalya B. has outshone everybody".

Filming

In the summer of 1970, the State Committee for Cinematography authorised the cinematic realisation of *Solaris*, with a length of 4,000 metres (13,123 ft), equivalent to two-hour-twenty-minute running time. The exteriors were photographed at Zvenigorod, near Moscow; the interiors were photographed at the Mosfilm studios. The scenes of space pilot Burton driving through a city were photographed in Japan, in September and October 1971, at Akasaka and Iikura in Tokyo. The shooting began in March 1971, by cinematographer Vadim Yusov, who also photographed Tarkovky's previous films. They frequently quarrelled to the degree of afterwards not working together again. The first version of *Solaris* was completed in December 1971.

Solaris locale: Akasaka, Tokyo, the future city that space pilot Henri Burton traverses in his car.

The Earth, the sensual source of life, and the sterile space station orbiting the planet Solaris, are contrasted with lively images of underwater plants, fire, snow, rain and other natural phenomena. A like contrast appears at story's end, on Solaris, juxtaposing Kelvin's winter visit to his father's house, featuring a frozen pond, surrounded by bare trees, but not covered with snow. The dead scenery contrasts with the earlier, summer pond scenes of underwater plants floating in the water current, and blooming trees. The Solaris ocean was created with acetone, aluminium powder, and dyes. Mikhail Romadin designed the space station as old and decrepit, rather than as futuristic. Designer and director consulted with, scientist and aerospace engineer, Lupichev, who lent them a mainframe computer for set decoration. Romadin designed a mirror room; the cameraman, Yusov, was hidden in a mirrored sphere. Akira Kurosawa, who was visiting the Mosfilm studios, was impressed with the space station design.

In January 1972 the State Committee for Cinematography requested editorial changes before releasing *Solaris*, such as a more realistic film with a clearer image of the future, and deletion of allusions to God and Christianity; Tarkovsky successfully resisted such major changes; yet, after some minor edits, *Solaris* was approved for release in March 1972.

Musical score

The soundtrack of *Solaris* features the chorale prelude for organ, *Ich ruf' zu dir, Herr Jesu Christ* (BWV 639), by Johan Sebastian Bach, and an electronic score by Eduard Artemyev. The prelude is the central musical theme of *Solaris*. Tarkovsky, initially, wanted a musicless film, and asked composer Artemyev to orchestrate the ambient sounds as a musical score. The latter proposed subtly introducing orchestral music. In counterpoint to the classical music Earth theme, is the fluid electronic music theme for the planet *Solaris*. The character of Hari has her own subtheme, a cantus firmus based upon J. S. Bach's music featuring Artemyev's composition atop it; it is heard at Hari's death and at story's end.

Reception and legacy

Although Stanisław Lem worked with Tarkovsky and Fridrikh Gorenshtein in developing the screenplay, Lem maintained that he "never really liked Tarkovsky's version" of his novel. Tarkovsky wanted a film story based on the novel but artistically independent of its origin. However, Lem opposed any divergence of the screenplay from the novel. Tarkovsky claimed that Lem did not fully appreciate cinema and that he expected the film to merely illustrate the novel without creating an original cinematic piece. Tarkovsky's film is about the inner lives of its scientists as human beings. Lem's novel is about the conflicts of man's condition in nature and the nature of man in the universe. For Tarkovsky, Lem's exposition of that existential conflict was the starting point for describing the inner lives of the characters.

In the autobiographical documentary *Voyage in Time* (1983), Tarkovsky says he viewed *Solaris* as an artistic failure because his film did not transcend genre like, he believed, his film *Stalker* (1979) did due to the required technological dialogue and special effects. M. Galina in the 1997 article *Identifying Fears* called this film "one of the biggest events in the Soviet science fiction cinema" and one of the few works that does not seem anachronistic nowadays.

Solaris premiered at the 1972 Cannes Film Festival and won the Grand Prix Spécial du Jury and was nominated for the Palme d'Or. In the USSR, the film premiered in the *Mir* film theater in Moscow on 5 February 1973. Tarkovsky did not consider the *Mir* cinema the best projection venue. Despite the film's narrow release in only five film theaters in the USSR, the film nevertheless sold 10.5 million tickets. Unlike the vast majority of commercial and ideological films in the 1970s, "Solaris" was screened in the USSR in limited copies for 15 years without any break, giving it cult status. In the Eastern Bloc and in the West, *Solaris* premiered later. In the United States, a version of *Solaris* that was truncated by 30 minutes premiered at the Ziegfeld Theatre in New York City on 6 October 1976.

A list of "The 100 Best Films Of World Cinema" compiled by *Empire* magazine in 2010 ranked Tarkovsky's *Solaris* at #68. In 2002, Steven Soderbergh wrote and directed an American adaptation of *Solaris*, which starred George Clooney.

Salman Rushdie calls *Solaris* "a sci-fi masterpiece", and has urged that "This exploration of the unreliability of reality and the power of the human unconscious, this great examination of the limits of rationalism and the perverse power of even the most ill-fated love, needs to be seen as widely as possible before it's transformed by Steven Soderbergh and James Cameron into what they ludicrously threaten will be '*2001* meets *Last Tango in Paris*.' What, sex in space with floating butter? Tarkovsky must be turning over in his grave."

Nimród Antal cites Solaris as one of the influences on the making of his first movie, Kontroll. Kontroll has many similarities with Solaris, such as the ambiguity of reality, the hallucinatory look, and the score, which also mixes both real instruments and electronic elements.

Source (edited): "http://en.wikipedia.org/wiki/Solaris_(1972_film)"

Stalker (film)

Stalker (Russian: Сталкер) is a 1979 science fiction film directed by Andrei Tarkovsky, with a screenplay written by Boris and Arkady Strugatsky, loosely based on their novel *Roadside Picnic*. It depicts an expedition led by the Stalker (guide) to bring his two clients to a site known as the Zone, which has the supposed potential to fulfil a person's innermost desires.

The title of the film, which is the same in Russian and English, is derived from the English word *to stalk* in the long-standing meaning of approaching furtively, much like a hunter. In the film a stalker is a professional guide to the zone, someone who crosses the border into the forbidden zone with a specific goal.

The sparseness of exposition leads to ambiguity as to the nature of The Zone.

Plot summary

The setting of the film is a tiny town on the outskirts of the Zone, a wilderness area which has been cordoned off by the government. The film's main character, the Stalker, works as a guide to bring people in and out of the Zone, to "the Room", which is said to grant the deepest, innermost wishes of anyone who steps inside. Residual effects of an undefined previous occurrence have transformed an otherwise mundane rural area scattered with ruined buildings into an area where the normal laws of physics no longer apply.

The film begins, in sepia, with the Stalker in his home with his wife and daughter. His wife emotionally urges him not to leave her again to go into the Zone because of the legal consequences, but he ignores her pleas. The Stalker goes to a bar, where he meets the Writer and the Professor, who will be his clients on his next trip into the Zone. The Writer and the Professor are never identified by name — the Stalker prefers to refer to them in this way. The three of them evade the military blockade that guards the Zone using a Land-Rover — attracting gunfire from the guards as they go — and then ride into the heart of the Zone on a railway work car. The camera follows their passage from urban setting to rural, and from the darkness required for their infiltration of the Zone, to light. This is also the point in the movie where the film switches to color.

The Stalker tells his clients that they must do exactly as he says to survive the dangers that, while invisible, are all around them. Although the Stalker describes extreme danger at all times, no harm comes to any of the three men; there is a tension between disbelief of the need for his elaborate precautions and the possibility that they are necessary. The Stalker tests various routes by throwing metal nuts tied with strips of cloth ahead of him before walking into a new area. The Zone appears peaceful and harmless. The Writer is skeptical that there is any real danger, while the Professor generally follows the Stalker's advice.

Much of the film focuses on the trip through the apparently dangerous Zone and the philosophical discussions that the characters share about their reasons for wanting to visit the Room. The Writer appears concerned that he is losing his inspiration, while the Professor apparently hopes to win a Nobel prize. Meanwhile, the Stalker — who explains that he has never gone into the Room himself — quotes from the New Testament and bemoans the loss of faith in society. Throughout the film, the Stalker refers to a previous Stalker, named "Porcupine," who led his poet brother to his death in the Zone, visited the Room and gained a lot of money, and then hanged himself. The implication is that our "deepest, innermost desires" are opaque even to ourselves, and the overt desire to win the lottery was coupled with the covert and unexpressed - perhaps unconscious - desire for his brother's death, and when Porcupine realized this, he killed himself to expiate his guilt. When the Writer confronts the Stalker about his knowledge of the Zone and the Room, he says that it all comes from Porcupine.

The trio first walk through meadows and then enter a tunnel that the Stalker calls "the meat grinder." In one of the decayed buildings, a phone inexplicably begins to ring. The Writer answers and says to whoever is on the other end that "this is not the clinic," and hangs up. The Professor then uses the phone to call a colleague. In the resultant conversation he reveals some of his true motives for having come to the Room. He has brought a bomb with him and intends to destroy the Room out of fear that it could be used for personal gain by evil men. The three men fight verbally and physically; the Professor backs down from his plan to destroy the Room. Their journey ends when they finally arrive at the entrance to the Room. A long take leaves the men sitting outside the Room, who then never enter it. Rain begins to fall from a dark sky where a ceiling once was, into the ruined building, and the rainstorm gradually fades away, all in one shot.

The next scene shows the Stalker, the Writer, and the Professor back in the bar. The Stalker's wife and child arrive. A mysterious black dog that followed the three men through the Zone is now in the bar with them. His wife asks where he got it; the Stalker says that it got attached to him and he could not leave it in the Zone. As the Stalker leaves the bar with his family and the dog, we see that his child, nicknamed "Monkey" is crippled, and cannot walk unaided. (Earlier dialogue has suggested that the child is affected by some form of genetic mutation as a "child of the Zone.") Later, when the Stalker's wife says she would like to visit the Room, he seems to have doubts about the Zone; he tells her he fears her dreams will not be fulfilled. While breaking the fourth wall, the Stalker's wife then contemplates her relationship with the Stalker, only to conclude that she is better off with him. The film ends with Monkey alone in the kitchen. She recites a poem by Fyodor Tyutchev and then lays her head on the table and appears to psychokinetically push three drinking glasses across the table, one after the other, with the last one falling to the floor. After the third glass falls to the floor, a train passes by (as in the beginning of the film), causing the entire apartment to shake.

Cast

- Alisa Freindlich as the Stalker's Wife
- Alexander Kaidanovsky as the Stalker
- Anatoli Solonitsyn as the Writer
- Nikolai Grinko as the Professor

Supporting actors:

- Natasha Abramova as Monkey, the Stalker's daughter
- F. Yurna, Y. Kostin and R. Rendi

Production

Writing

The film is loosely based on the novel *Roadside Picnic* by Boris and Arkady Strugatsky. After reading the novel, initially Tarkovsky recommended it to his friend, the film director Mikhail Kalatozov, thinking that he might be interested in adapting it into a film. Kalatozov, however, could not obtain the rights to the film from the Strugatsky brothers and abandoned the project. Tarkovsky then began to be more and more interested in adapting the novel. He hoped that it would allow him to make a film that conforms to the classical Aristotelian unity, that is the unity of action, the unity of location and the unity of time.

The film departs considerably from the novel. According to Tarkovsky the film has nothing in common with the novel except for the two words Stalker and Zone.

An early draft of the screenplay was published as a novel *Stalker* that differs much from the finished film. In *Roadside Picnic* the site was specifically described as the site of alien visitation; the name of the novel derives from a metaphor proposed by a character who compares the visit to a roadside picnic. After the picnickers depart, nervous animals venture forth from the adjacent forest and discover the picnic garbage: spilled motor oil, faded unknown flowers, a box of matches, a clockwork teddy bear, balloons, candy wrappers. He concludes that the Zone is to humankind as the picnic's leftovers are to the forest animals; what the aliens carelessly toss aside is beyond our understanding and a source of power and danger.

In an interview on the MK2 DVD, production designer Rashit Safiullin describes the Zone as a space in which humans can live without the trappings of society and can speak about the most important things freely.

Some elements of the original novel remain. In *Roadside Picnic*, the Zone is full of strange artifacts and phenomena that defy known science. A vestige of this idea carries over to the film, in the form of Stalker's habit of throwing metal nuts down a path before walking along it; the characters in *Roadside Picnic* do something similar when they suspect they are near gravitational anomalies that could crush them.

In another sharp contrast, the penultimate scene of the movie is a first person monologue by the Stalker's wife, where she looks directly into the camera and explains, with increasing authority, how she met the Stalker and decided to stick with him. It is the only such scene in the entire 160 minutes of the film; the content though is a kind of answer to what the same woman had said in the opening scene, when she blamed her husband for their miseries. It carries clear allusions to Christ (who also called strangers to "follow me") and as some reviewers pointed out, echoes the style of 19th-century Russian novels with their bold and passionate heroines.

Production

In an interview on the MK2 DVD, the production designer, Rashit Safiullin, recalls that Tarkovsky spent a year shooting a version of the outdoor scenes of *Stalker*. However, when the crew got back to Moscow, they found that all of the film had been improperly developed and their footage was unusable. The film had been shot on experimental Kodak stock with which Soviet laboratories were unfamiliar.

Even before the film stock problem was discovered, relations between Tarkovsky and the first cinematographer, Georgy Rerberg, had been in serious deterioration. After seeing the poorly developed material, Rerberg left the first screening session and never came back. By the time the film stock defect was discovered, Tarkovsky had shot all the outdoor scenes and had to burn them. Safiullin contends that Tarkovsky was so despondent that he wanted to abandon further production of the film.

After the loss of the film stock, the Soviet film boards wanted to shut the film down, officially writing it off. But Tarkovsky came up with a solution: he asked to make a two-part film, which meant additional deadlines and more funds. Tarkovsky ended up reshooting almost all of the film with a new cinematographer, Aleksandr Knyazhinsky. According to Safiullin, the finished version of *Stalker* is completely different from the one Tarkovsky originally shot.

The film mixes sepia and color footage; within the Zone, in the countryside, all is colorful, while the outside, urban world is tinted sepia.

One of the deserted hydro power plants near Jägala Waterfall, recently renovated

The central part of the film, in which the characters move around the Zone, was shot in a few days at two deserted hydro power plants on the Jägala river near Tallinn, Estonia. The shot before they enter the Zone is an old Flora chemical factory in the center of Tallinn, next to the old Rotermann salt storage and the electric plant—now a culture factory where a memorial plate of the film has been set up in 2008. Some shots from the Zone were filmed in Maardu, next to the Iru powerplant, while the shot with the gates to the Zone was filmed in Lasnamäe, next to Punane Street behind the Idakeskus. Some shots were filmed near the Tallinn-Narva highway bridge on the Pirita River.

The documentary film *Rerberg and Tarkovsky: The Reverse Side of "Stalker"* by Igor Mayboroda sheds new light on the production of "Stalker". The relation between Rerberg and Tarkovsky suffered tremendously during the production of "Stalker". Rerberg felt that Tarkovsky was not ready for this script. He told Tarkovsky to rewrite the script in order to achieve a good result. Tarkovsky ignored him and continued shooting. After several arguments, Tarkovsky sent Rerberg home. Ultimately, Tarkovsky shot this movie three times, consuming over 5,000 meters of film. People who have seen both the first version shot by Rerberg (as Director of Photography) and the final theatrical release say that they are almost identical. Tarkovsky sent home other crew members in addition to Rerberg and excluded them from the ending credits as well. Many people involved in the film production had untimely deaths, which were attributed to the long, arduous shooting schedule of the film as well as to toxins present at the shooting locations. Vladimir Sharun recalls:

We were shooting near Tallinn in the area around the small river Jägala with a half-functioning hydroelectric station. Up the river was a chemical plant and it poured out poisonous liquids downstream. There is even this shot in Stalker: snow falling in the summer and white foam floating down the river. In fact it was some horrible poison. Many women in our crew got allergic reactions on their faces. Tarkovsky died from cancer of the right bronchial tube. And Tolya Solonitsyn too. That it was all connected to the location shooting for Stalker became clear to me when Larisa Tarkovskaya died from the same illness in Paris.

Cinematography

Like Tarkovsky's other films, *Stalker* relies on long takes with slow, subtle camera movement, rejecting the conventional use of rapid montage. Almost all of the shots not set in the Zone are in a high-contrast brown monochrome.

The film contains not more than 142 shots in 163 minutes with an average shot length of almost one minute and many shots lasting for more than four minutes.

The *Stalker* film score was composed by Eduard Artemyev, who had also composed the film scores for Tarkovsky's previous films *Solaris* and *The Mirror*. For *Stalker* Artemyev composed and recorded two different versions of the score. The first score was done with an orchestra alone but was rejected by Tarkovsky. The second score that was used in the final film was created on a synthesizer along with traditional instruments that were manipulated using sound effects. In the final film score the boundaries between music and sound were blurred, as natural sounds and music interact to the point were they are indistinguishable. In fact, many of the natural sounds were not production sounds but were created by Artemyev on his synthesizer. For Tarkovsky music was more than just a parallel illustration of the visual image. He believed that music distorts and changes the emotional tone of a visual image while not changing the meaning. He also believed that in a film with complete theoretical consistency music will have no place and that instead music is replaced by sounds. According to Tarkovsky, he aimed at this consistency and moved into this direction in *Stalker* and *Nostalghia*.

In addition to the original monophonic soundtrack a newer, alternative soundtrack remixed in 5.1 surround sound exists. This alternative soundtrack was created for the 2001 DVD release by the Russian Cinema Council (Ruscico). Apart from remixing the mono soundtrack into stereo surround sound, music and sound effects were removed and added in several scenes. Music was added to the scene where the three are traveling to the zone on a motorized draisine. In the opening and the final scene Beethoven's *Ninth Symphony* was removed and in the opening scene in Stalker's house ambient sounds were added, changing the original soundtrack, in which this scene was completely silent except for the sound of a train.

Film score

Initially Tarkovsky had no clear understanding of the musical atmosphere of the final film and only an approximate idea where in the film the music was to be. Even after he had shot all the material he continued his search for the ideal film score, wanting a combination of Oriental and Western music. In a conversation with Artemyev he explained that he needed music that reflects the idea that although the East and the West can coexist, they are not able to understand each other. One of Tarkovsky's ideas was to perform Western music on Oriental instruments, or vice versa, performing Oriental music on European instruments. Artemyev proposed to try this idea with the motet *Pulcherrima Rosa* by an anonymous 14th century Italian composer dedicated to the Virgin Mary. In its original form Tarkovsky did not perceive the motet as suitable for the film and asked Artemyev to give it an Oriental sound. Later, Tarkovsky proposed to invite musicians from Armenia and Azerbaijan and to let them improvise on the melody of the motet. A musician was invited from Armenia who played the main melody on a tar, accompanied by orchestral background music written by Artemyev. Tarkovsky, who, unusually for him, attended the full recording session, rejected the final result as not what he was looking for.

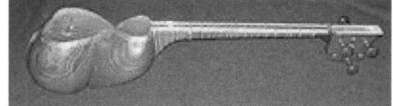

A tar, a traditional Persian instrument that is also common in the Caucasus is used in the Stalker theme.

Rethinking their approach they finally found the solution in a theme that would create a state of inner calmness and inner satisfaction, or as Tarkovsky said "space frozen in a dynamic equilibrium." Artemyev knew about a musical piece from Indian classical music where a prolonged and unchanged background tone is performed on a tambura. As this gave Artemyev the impression of frozen space, he used this inspiration and created a background tone on his synthesizer similar to the background tone performed on the tambura. The tar then improvised on the background sound, together with a flute as a European, Western instrument. To mask the obvious combination of European and Oriental instruments he passed the foreground music through the effect channels of his SYNTHI 100 synthesizer. These effects included modulating the sound of the flute and lowering the speed of the tar, so that what Artemyev called "the life of one string" could be heard. Tarkovsky was amazed by the result, especially liking the sound of the tar, and used the theme without any alterations in the film.

Sound design

The title sequence is accompanied by Artemyev's main theme. The opening sequence of the film showing Stalker's room is mostly silent. Periodically one hears what could be a train. The sound becomes louder and clearer over time until the sound and the vibrations of objects in the room give a sense of a train's passing by without the train's being visible. This aural impression is quickly subverted by the muffled sound of Beethoven's *Ninth Symphony*. The source of this music is unclear, thus setting the tone for the blurring of reality in the film. For this part of the film Tarkovsky was also considering music by Richard Wagner or the *Marseillaise*. In an interview with Tonino Guerra Tarkovsky said that he wanted "music that is more or less popular, that expresses the movement of the masses, the theme of humanity's social destiny. But this music must be barely heard beneath the noise, in a way that the spectator is not aware of it.". As the sound of the train becomes more and more distant, the sounds of the house, such as the creaking floor, water running through pipes, and the humming of a heater become more prominent. While the Stalker leaves his house and wanders around an industrial landscape, the audience hears industrial sounds such as train whistles, ship foghorns, and train wheels. When the Stalker, the Writer, and the Professor set off from the bar in an off-road vehicle, the engine noise merges into an electronic tone. The natural sound of the engine falls off as the vehicle reaches the horizon. Initially almost inaudible, the electronic tone emerges and replaces the engine sound as if time has frozen.

"I would like most of the noise and sound to be composed by a composer. In the film, for example, the three people undertake a long journey in a railway car. I'd like that the noise of the wheels on the rails not be the natural sound but elaborated upon by the composer with electronic music. At the same time, one mustn't be aware of music, nor natural sounds."
Andrei Tarkovsky in an interview with Tonino Guerra in 1979.

The journey to the Zone on a motorized draisine features a disconnection between the visual image and the sound. The presence of the draisine is registered only through the clanking sound of the wheels on the tracks. Neither the draisine nor the scenery passing by is shown, since the camera is focused on the faces of the characters. This disconnection draws the audience into the inner world of the characters and transforms the physical journey into an inner journey. This effect on the audience is reinforced by Artemyev's synthesizer effects, which make the clanking wheels sound less and less natural as the journey progresses. When the three arrive in the Zone initially, it appears to be silent. Only after some time, and only slightly audibly can one hear the sound of a distant river, the sound of the blowing wind, or the occasional cry of an animal. These sounds grow richer and more audible while the Stalker makes his first venture into the Zone, initially leaving the professor and the writer behind, and as if the sound draws him towards the zone. The sparseness of sounds in the zone draws attention to specific sounds, which, as in other scenes, are largely disconnected from the visual image. Animals can be heard in the distance but are never shown. A breeze can be heard, but no visual reference is shown. This effect is reinforced by occasional synthesizer effects which meld with the natural sounds and blur the boundaries between artificial and alien sounds and the sounds of nature.

After the three travelers appear from the tunnel, the sound of dripping water can be heard. While the camera slowly pans to the right, a waterfall appears. While the visual transition of the panning shot is slow, the aural transition is sudden. As soon as the waterfall appears, the sound of the dripping water falls off while the thundering sound of the waterfall emerges, almost as if time has jumped. In the next scene Tarkovsky again uses the technique of disconnecting sound and visual image. While the camera pans over the burning ashes of a fire and over some water, the audience hears the conversation of the Stalker and the Writer who are back in the tunnel looking for the professor. Finding the Professor outside, the three are surprised to realize that the have ended up at an earlier point in time. This and the previous disconnection of sound and the visual image illustrate the Zone's power to alter time and space. This technique is even more evident in the next scene where the three travelers are resting. The sounds of a river, the wind, dripping water, and fire can be heard in a discontinuous way that is now partially disconnected from the visual image. When the Professor, for example, extinguishes the fire by throwing his coffee on it, all sounds but that of the dripping water fall off. Similarly, we can hear and see the Stalker and the river. Then the camera cuts back to the Professor while the audience can still hear the river for a few more seconds. This impressionist use of sound prepares the audience for the dream sequences accompanied by a variation of the Stalker theme that has been already heard during the title sequence.

During the journey in the Zone, the sound of water becomes more and more prominent, which, combined with the visual image, presents the zone as a drenched world. In an interview Tarkovsky dismissed the idea that water has a symbolic meaning in his films, saying that there was so much rain in his films because it is always raining in

Russia. In another interview, on the film *Nostalghia*, however, he said "Water is a mysterious element, a single molecule of which is very photogenic. It can convey movement and a sense of change and flux." Emerging from the tunnel called the meat grinder by the Stalker they arrive at the entrance of their destination, the room. Here, as in the rest of the film, sound is constantly changing and not necessarily connected to the visual image. The journey in the Zone ends with the three sitting in the room, silent, with no audible sound. When the sound resumes, it is again the sound of water but with a different timbre, softer and gentler, as if to give a sense of catharsis and hope. The transition back to the world outside the zone is supported by sound. While the camera still shows a pool of water inside the Zone, the audience begins to hear the sound of a train and Ravel's *Boléro*, reminiscent of the opening scene. The soundscape of the world outside the zone is the same as before, characterized by train wheels, foghorns of a ship and train whistles. The film ends as it began, with the sound of a train passing by, accompanied by the muffled sound of Beethoven's *Ninth symphony*, this time the *Ode to Joy* from the final moments of the symphony. As in the rest of the film the disconnect between the visual image and the sound leaves the audience in the unclear whether the sound is real or an illusion.

Distribution

Stalker sold 4.3 million tickets in the Soviet Union.

DVD

- In GDR DEFA did a complete German synchronization of the movie which was shown in cinema 1982. This was used by Icestorm Entertainment on a DVD release, but was heavily criticized for its lack of the original language version, subtitles and had an overall bad image quality.
- RUSCICO produced a version for the international market containing the film on two DVDs with remastered audio and video. It contains the original Russian audio in a enhanced Dolby Digital 5.1-remix as well as the original mono version. The DVD also contains subtitles in 13 languages and interviews with Alexander Knyazhinsky, Rashit Safiullin and Edward Artemiev.

Reception

Officials at Goskino were critical of the film, on being told that the film should be faster and more dynamic, Tarkovsky replied:

" the film needs to be slower and duller at the start so that the viewers who walked into the wrong theatre have time to leave before the main action starts. "

The Goskino representative then explained that he was trying to give the point of view of the audience. Tarkovsky supposedly retorted:

" I am only interested in the views of two people: one is called Bresson and one called Bergman. "

The Western Reception has been a little timid, the movie was slowly made available and since it was after the release the reviews were not concurrent, nevertheless, it currently holds 100% positive reviews on Rotten Tomatoes.

Film critic Derek Adams compared *Stalker* to Francis Ford Coppola's *Apocalypse Now* also released in 1979, "as a journey to the heart of darkness, [Stalker] is a good deal more persuasive than Coppola's."

Influence

Seven years after the making of the film, the Chernobyl accident led to the depopulation of an area rather like that in the film. Some of those employed to take care of the abandoned nuclear power plant refer to themselves as "stalkers" and to the area around the damaged reactor as "The Zone."

Although not an official connection, the 2007 Ukrainian PC game *S.T.A.L.K.E.R.: Shadow of Chernobyl* borrowed several elements from the film. The game's Anomalies and Artifacts are analogous to the enhanced gravity fields in *Stalker*, while the golden globe featured in *Roadside Picnic* and the room in Stalker are represented in the game by "Wish Granter", a huge object in the destroyed reactor hall of the Chernobyl nuclear plant, which has wish-granting abilities. The cause is a second disaster in Chernobyl, not alien contact, although it is heavily implied that the monolith is a result of alien interference. "The Zone" is used to describe the area affected by Chernobyl. Other similarities between the film and the game are the throwing of nuts and bolts to find safe passage through the zone, and a forever present threat portrayed in both film and game of invisible threats and pitfalls.

Hommage

- David Bate's 2001 photographs called 'Zone', shot in and round Tallinn explicitly refers to Stalker, the story and the location of the film. He uses metaphorical language to link the zone in Stalker to the situation of the post-Soviet situation, where 'alien' rules of desire (market economies) now govern these spaces.
- Chris Marker, in his 1982 film *Sans Soleil*, refers to Tarkovsky's *Stalker* through the use of the term "Zone" to describe the space in which images and their attached memories are transformed.
- Björk's song "The Dull Flame of Desire" (released on her 2007 album *Volta*) takes as its lyrics an English translation of the Fyodor Tyutchev poem that appears at the end of the film. In the album booklet she mentions the film as the source of the poem.
- Towards the end of the track "Requiem For Dying Mothers, Part 2" on the album The Tired Sounds of Stars of the Lid by Stars Of The Lid (released in 2001), the soundtrack of the final scene in the film - where Monkey pushes the glass across the table by way of telekinesis as the dog whines and a foghorn is heard in the distance - is sampled and dubbed

into the track.
- Brian Lustmord and Robert Rich collaborated to compose an album, also titled *Stalker*, which was released in 1995 and was inspired by the film.
- Techno artist Richie Hawtin in his DVD version of 2005 mix album "DE9: Transitions", features a somewhat distorted final scene from the film - where Monkey pushes the glass across the table, while the track "We (All) Search" of the artist is playing, in synchronization with video. This is later followed by a similar scene, where the artist himself is sitting by the white table, while mentally interacting with geometrical shapes in front of him. At the end, he leans on the table just like Monkey. The track "The Tunnel" is playing in the background.
- Jacek Kaczmarski recorded a song 'Stalker', whose lyrics are heavily influenced by Tarkovsky's film.
- Orchestral Manoeuvres in the Dark recorded 'The Avenue', which is centered around a sample of the handcar in the film.
- In the 1992 independent film In the Soup a poster for the film can be seen in Aldolfo (Steve Buscemi)'s apartment.
- In the 2002 film Uzak (Distant), by Turkish film director Nuri Bilge Ceylan, the handcar scene is featured on a TV in the background.

Source (edited): "http://en.wikipedia.org/wiki/Stalker_(film)"

Teens in the Universe

Teens in the Universe (Russian: Отроки во вселенной, translit. *Otroki vo vselennoy*) is a Soviet 1974 film directed by Richard Viktorov based on a script by Isai Kuznetsov and Avenir Zak. Preceded by Moscow-Cassiopeia (first part, 1973). Runtime - 84 min.

Cast
- Innokenti Smoktunovsky as *I.O.O.*
- Vasili Merkuryev as *academician Blagovidov*
- Lev Durov as *academician Filatov*
- Yuri Medvedev as *academician Ogon-Duganovsky*
- Pyotr Merkuryev as *academician Kurochkin*

Space ship *Zarya* crew
- Mikhail Yershov as *Sereda*
- Aleksandr Grigoryev as *Kozelkov*
- Vladimir Savin as *Kopanygin*
- Vladimir Basov Jr. as *Lobanov*
- Olga Bityukova as *Kuteishchikova*
- Nadezhda Ovcharova as *Sorokina*
- Irina Popova as *Panfyorova*

Other cast
- Vadim Ledogorov as *Agapit*
- Igor Ledogorov as *Agapit's father*
- Natalya Fateyeva
- Anatoli Adoskin
- Aleksandr Lenkov
- Nikolai Pogodin
- Raisa Ryazanova
- S. Safonov
- Nadezhda Semyontsova
- Vladimir Shiryayev
- Olga Soshnikova
- Aleksandr Vigdorov
- Mikhail Yanushkevich
- Aleksandr Zimin

Awards
- Premio for the Best Film for Kids and Youth of the All-Union Cinema Festival, Kishinev, 1975
- Special Premio "Silver Asteroid" of the International Cinema Festival of Science Fiction Films, Triest, 1976
- Gran Premio of the International Festival at Panama, 1976
- State Premio of RSFSR in the honour of Vasilyiev Brothers, 1977.

Source (edited): "http://en.wikipedia.org/wiki/Teens_in_the_Universe"

Test pilota Pirxa

Inquest of Pilot Pirx (Polish: *Test pilota Pirxa*, Russian: Дознание пилота Пиркса, translit. Doznanie pilota Pirksa, Estonian: *Navigaator Pirx*) is a joint Polish//Estonian/Ukrainian 1978 film directed by Marek Piestrak based on the story *The Inquest* by Stanisław Lem from his short story collection More Tales of Pirx the Pilot. It was adapted for film by Vladimir Valutsky. It is a joint production by Dovzhenko Film Studios, Tallinnfilm, and Zespol Filmowy. Music by Arvo Pärt, sound by Aleksandr Gołębiowski, cinematography by Janusz Pawlowski. Runtime 104 min.

Plot summary

This movie is about a rocket pilot named Pirx who is hired to go on a mission to evaluate some nonlinears (robots) for use as crewmembers on future space flights. Pirx and his crew, made up of nonlinears and humans, are sent out to launch two satellites into the rings of Saturn. There is a near disaster and the human crew are almost killed. Upon returning to Earth there is an inquest to determine if Pirx was responsible for the "accident." In the end, it is found that one of the robots caused the malfunction in an attempt to kill the human crewmembers and Pirx is cleared of all charges.

In this tale Lem puts forth the idea that what is perceived a human weakness is in fact an advantage over a perfect machine. Pirx defeats the robot, because a human can hesitate, make wrong decisions, have doubts, but a robot cannot. A similar idea is present in Isaac Asimov's Robot Series, where putting a robot in a position where it cannot chose between the Three laws of robotics fries its positronic brain.

Differences between the story and the movie

The biggest difference is the fact that the movie tells the story in chronological order with the inquest taking place at the end while the short story starts with the inquest and then goes back in time from there. The movie also includes an assassination attempt on Pirx to prevent him from accepting the mission while this is not present in the short story. Another difference is that in the movie Pirx and his crew are attempting to launch two satellites into Saturn's rings while in the short story they are trying to launch three.

Cast

- Sergei Desnitsky as *Commandor Pirx*
- Aleksandr Kaidanovsky as *Tom Nowak*, neurologist and cyberneticist
- Vladimir Ivashov as *Harry Brown*, 2nd Pilot
- Tõnu Saar as *Kurt Weber*, nucleonicist engineer
- Aleksandr Belyavskiy
- Igor Przegrodzki as *McGuirr*
- Boleslaw Abart as *Jan Otis*, electronicist
- Janusz Bylczynski as *Juge*
- Mieczysław Janowski as *Mitchell*
- Jerzy Kaliszewski as *Dr. Kristoff*
- Zbigniew Lesien as *John Calder*, 1st Pilot
- Ferdynand Matysik as *Green*, the UNESCO Director

Reception

Test pilota Pirxa was awarded the "Golden Asteroid" Big Prize on the XVIII International Cinema Festival at Triest 1979.

Source (edited): "http://en.wikipedia.org/wiki/Test_pilota_Pirxa"

The Adventures of the Elektronic

The Adventures of Elektronik (Russian: Приключения Электроника, translit. Priklyucheniya Elektronika) is a 1980 Soviet adventure TV miniseries directed by Konstantin Bromberg.

Novel and screenplay by Yevgeni Veltistov. His fiction novels "Elektronic - the boy from the suitcase" (1964) and "Ressi - an elusive friend" (1971) were adapted into three film series by Bromberg. The TV premiere was on 2 May 1980. The film achieved a cult status among the Soviet kids.

Plot summary

A robot named Elektronic escapes from Professor Gromov's laboratory. The robot looks exactly like Sergey (Serezha) Syroezhkin, the boy from the magazine cover, which was chosen by Gromov as a model to construct Elektronic.

By coincidence, the double meets its prototype. 6-grader Serezha cunningly suggests that Elektronik should impersonate him - go to school instead of him and even live in his home. His plan works, as no one can tell the difference between them. Serezha's teachers delight in a very gifted pupil, who suddenly shows unbelievable talents in math, gymnastics, drawing and even singing. Sergey's parents do not suspect his trick and are glad of their pseudo-son's progress.

However, eventually the boy realizes that as the robot takes over "his" life, he may be out of business...

At the same time, "somewhere abroad", a gang of criminals operates. It is headed by a criminal authority known as Stump. He tells Urrie, who is the best in their gang, to find and kidnap Elektronic. They want to organize a "crime of the century" with the use of his extraordinary abilities.

Cast

- Yuri Torsuyev as *Syroyezhkin*
- Vladimir Torsuyev as *Elektronic*
- Vasili Skromny as *Gusev*
- Oksana Alekseyeva as *Maika*
- Maksim Kalinin as *Korol'kov*
- Dmitri Maksimov as *Smirnov*
- Yevgeni Livshits as *Ryzhikov/Chizhikov*
- Valeriya Soluyan as *Kukushkina*
- Vladimir Basov as *Stump*
- Nikolai Karachentsov as *Urrie*
- Nikolai Grinko as *Professor Gromov*
- Yelizaveta Nikishchikhina as *Masha*, Gromov's assistant
- Yevgeny Vesnik as *Tarator'*, the math teacher
- Maya Bulgakova as *School's headmistress*
- Nikolai Boyarsky as *Rostik*, the gymnastics teacher
- Roza Makagonova, the singing lessons teacher
- Nataliya Vasazhenko, Syroyezhkin's mother
- Yuri Chernov, Syroyezhkin's father
- Lev Perfilov as *Lyug*, Stump's gangster
- Gennadi Yalovich as *Bree*, Stump's gangster

Originally, it was planned that both Syroyezhkin and Elektronic roles would be played by just one boy. But the director of the film decided to simplify the filming process by using twins. His assistants screened a hundred twins throughout most of the Soviet Union. One of the casting days took place in the winter, when the temperature was below zero, nobody came except for the Torsuyev brothers. It was they who were cast in leading roles. In test filmings, Yuri played the role of Elektronic and Vladimir of Syroyezhkin, but the roles were later changed by the director. During the filming period the kids grew up too fast, and it was necessary to make new costumes from time to time.

Music

Music for the film were written by Evgeni Krylatov. His lyrics was perform in the film by Elena Kamburova, Elena Shuenkova and the chorus; no actors, except for Karachentsov and Basov, were afforded an opportunity to sing. (The lyrics were written by Jury Entin)

Source (edited): "http://en.wikipedia.org/wiki/The_Adventures_of_the

_Elektronic"

The Andromeda Nebula

The Andromeda Nebula (Russian: Туманность Андромеды) is a 1967 Russian Science fiction film starring Sergei Stolyarov and directed by Yevgeni Sherstobitov. The film was originally intended to be the first episode of a series of films but the remaining parts were never made. De facto name — *The Andromeda Nebula: Episode I. Prisoners of the Iron Star.*

Plot

It is based upon the *Andromeda Nebula* novel by Ivan Yefremov and follows the story of a group of humans on the spaceship *Tantra* who are tasked with investigating an unexplored area of space. During the course of the voyage the ship is trapped by the gravitational force of an Iron Star and is held in place for 20 years. Surrounded by predators who eat human flesh through clothing one by one the crew begin to fall prey with the only source of protection being the light from Tantra which has the ability to scare away the predators.

Source (edited): "http://en.wikipedia.org/wiki/The_Andromeda_Nebula"

The Hyperboloid of Engineer Garin (film)

The Hyperboloid of Engineer Garin (Russian: Гиперболоид инженера Гарина, translit. Giperboloid inzhenera Garina) also abberivated as **Engineer Garin** is a black-and-white 1965 Soviet science fiction film based on Aleksey Tolstoy's novel *The Garin Death Ray*.

Awards

- IFF of Fantasy Films in Trieste (Italy) – Top Prize "Golden Seal of the City of Trieste", 1966

Cast

- Yevgeniy Yevstigneyev as *Pyotr Petrovich Garin* (*Engineer Garin*)
- Vsevolod Safonov as *Vasily Shelga*
- Mikhail Astangov as *Mr. Rolling*
- Natalya Klimova as *Zoya Montrose*
- Vladimir Druzhnikov as *Arthur Levy / Volshin*
- Mikhail Kuznetsov as *Hlynov*
- Yurij Sarantsev as *Tarashkin*
- Nikolai Bubnov as *Nikolai Mantsev*
- Viktor Chekmaryov as *Four-fingered*
- Pavel Shpringfeld as *Gaston / Duck Nose*
- Bruno O'Ya as *Captain Yansen*
- Alyosha Ushakov as *Vanya Gusev*
- Anatoly Romashin as *Dr. Wolf*
- Valentin Bryleyev as *Victor Lenoir*
- Artyom Karapetyan as *secretary*
- Vyacheslav Gostinsky as *comandant of the Golden Isalnd*
- Stepan Krylov as *telegraph worker*
- Vladimir Balashov as *scientist (episode)*
- Konstantin Karelsky

Source (edited): "http://en.wikipedia.org/wiki/The_Hyperboloid_of_Engineer_Garin_(film)"

The Mystery of the Third Planet

The Mystery of the Third Planet (Russian: Тайна третьей планеты, *Tayna tretyey planety*), aka **The Secret of the Third Planet** is a 1981 Soviet traditionally-animated feature film directed by Roman Kachanov and produced by the Soyuzmultfilm studio in Moscow. It is based on one of a series of stories by well-known writer Kir Bulychyov about Alisa (Alice) Seleznyova, a young girl living in the second half of the 22nd century in a communist society (though no aspects of communism are mentioned or shown in the film).

In United States voiced by Kirsten Dunst as Alisa and James Belushi as Govorun.

Plot

On June 2, 2181, Alice, her father Professor Seleznyov and Captain Green go on a space expedition to find rare animals for Moscow Zoo. On the way, they visit many planets, meet many interesting denizens of the cosmos (such as a flying cow and a chatterbird) and accidentally uncover and become caught up in a criminal conspiracy.

Home video and English adaptations

The film was adapted twice for the US market. It was first brought over as a video release in 1987, with dubbed voices. The second time, it was released in the 1990s as part of Mikhail Baryshnikov's "Stories from My Childhood" series. This series consisted of films that were bought by California-based company Films by Jove from Soyuzmultfilm for the international market. Over $1.5 million was spent by this company restoring the prints, adding new music and redubbing the films with American actors. This version of the film was named *Alice and the Mystery of the Third Planet* and has been released on VHS as well as on a 1999 DVD collection with several other films . The film has been released on DVD several times (the latest release, which featured rather misleading cover art, was in October 2005), but there is currently no version which preserves the original

Russian voices and music and also has English subtitles. The Films by Jove version of the film has been criticized by some of those who saw the original for adding many extra dialogue lines, shortening the film, and replacing the unique synthesizer music by Alexander Zatsepin.

The original film has been released on several DVD editions in Russia, including a newly-restored one by Krupnyy Plan.

Games

- In 2005 an arcade platform game was made by the company Akella based on the film, called "Alice's Space Adventure".
- An adventure game was released in the same year called "Alice's Journey", also produced by Akella (but developed by "Step Creative Group").

Source (edited): "http://en.wikipedia.org/wiki/The_Mystery_of_the_Third_Planet"

The Sannikov Land (film)

The Sannikov Land (Russian: Земля Санникова, *Zemlya Sannikova*; Finnish: *Salattu maa*) is a Soviet 1973 adventure film about the fictional Sannikov Land based on the novel with the same name by Vladimir Obruchev.

Cast

- Vladislav Dvorzhetsky as *Ilyin*
- Oleg Dal as *Evgeniy Krestovskiy*
- Yuri Nazarov as *Gubin*
- Georgi Vitsin as *Ignatiy*
- Makhmud Esambayev as *Shaman*
- Nikolai Gritsenko
- Alyona Chukhraj
- Gevork Chepchyan
- Pyotr Abasheyev
- Tursun Kuralyev
- Yekaterina Sambuyeva
- Nasira Mambetova
- Sergei Polezhayev
- Aleksandr Susnin
- Nikolai Kryukov
- Boris Gryzlov

Soundtracks

Film featured two highly popular songs, written by Aleksandr Zatsepin and Leonid Derbenyov and performed by Oleg Anofriyev. First of them achieved nearly a cult status:

- "There's just a blink..." ("Est' tol'ko mig")
- "All has been" ("Vsyo bylo")

Source (edited): "http://en.wikipedia.org/wiki/The_Sannikov_Land_(film)"

The Witches Cave

The Witches Cave (Russian: Подземелье ведьм) was a 1989 science fiction, fantasy film from Gorky Film Studio, USSR and Barrandov Studios, Czechoslovakia.

The film scenarion was written by Kir Bulychev based upon his own story and directed by Yuri Moroz. The cast featured Sergei Zhigunov as Andrei Bruce, Marina Levtova as Belogurochka Dmitri Pevtsov as Oktin Khash and Nikolai Karachentsov as cosmolinguist Jean.

Plot summary

An interstellar expedition is sent to study a strange planet far from Earth. Despite the fact that creatures from various Earth time periods appear to inhabit the world (mammoths, pterodactyls, dinosaurs, horses, birds, etc.), the stone-age-level natives also possess swords made of metal, even though their civilization should have no knowledge of such advanced weaponry.

Source (edited): "http://en.wikipedia.org/wiki/The_Witches_Cave"